Cyprian of Antioch
A Mage of Many Faces

by Frater Acher

For more information, please visit www.quareia.com and theomagica.com

Copyright 2017 © Frater Acher

All rights reserved

Without limiting the rights under copyright reserved above, no part of this publication may be reproduced, stored in, or introduced into a retrieval system, or transmitted, in any form or by any means (electronic, mechanical, photocopying, recording or otherwise) without prior permission of the copyright owner and the publisher of this book.

First Edition printed 2017

Published by Quareia Publishing UK

ISBN 978-1-911134-27-5

Cover image and icon by Stuart Littlejohn

Typeset and copyedited by Michael Sheppard

Contents

Overview   7

Preface   9

Introduction   15

1   Cyprian the Ancient   25
    From Antioch to Rome:
        a secret ritual chamber 29
    Via Piacenza to Milan:
        the urn of St. Cyprian 49
    Conclusion 58

2   Cyprian of Two Worlds   61
    The Oratio Cypriani:
        blessing the lineage 61
    Conclusion 100
    The Grimoire of Cyprian:
        a Coptic erotic love spell 106
    Conclusion 117

3　Cyprian of Folk Magic　　　121
The Mirror of Cyprianus,
  by Theodor Storm, 1862 127
Three Wicked Tongues:
  Cyprian of the Flesh 175
Ilsenburg & Olsborg:
  Cyprian of the Northern past 190

4　Cyprian of the Mysteries　　　211
The Many Faces of Divination 213
Example 1:
  Binding the Mage's Spirit into the Mirror . 225
Example 2:
  Working with the Empty Hand 237
Conclusion 272

5　Cyprian of Cyprus　　　273
The Great Female Divine 274
Conclusion 289

Afterword　　　297

Bibliography　　　299

Overview

This book was written with the advanced student of Western magic and mysticism in mind. Many terms, such as 'magic,' 'vision,' 'demon,' and 'inner and outer realms,' will be left unexplained, it being assumed that they are familiar to the reader from their studies both theoretical *and* practical. The histories, legends, and spiritual traditions surrounding Cyprian of Antioch will also be assumed to be familiar territory, as a general introduction to them can easily be found online or in many of the recent publications on the subject.

This book hopes to offer the reader some new perspectives on Cyprian of Antioch, and to provide access to some less well-known Cyprianic material. It cites its sources and includes a bibliography, so the interested reader should find it easy to take up their own researches after they have finished this book.

Hopefully, it will also illustrate how working with a spirit of the Western magical tradition does not always require traditional forms of practice, and how it can lead one into previously unexplored territory and help one discover hidden—i.e. occult—access points to the spiritual force with which one is collaborating. Indeed, this book itself is a direct expression of my personal work with Cyprian of Antioch, and its production was work in service to him.

LVX, Frater Acher.
Munich, 2017.

Preface

How many stories are waiting to be told about Cyprian of Antioch? How many names do we know for this myth of a man? Cyprian the Mage, Cyprian the Saint, Cyprian of the North, Cyprian of the Iberian Peninsula, Cyprian of the New World... There is a seemingly endless succession of iterations retelling the story that first cast its shadow over the world of fourth-century Christendom. And though this world was quickly sanitized, Cyprian's shadow stuck fast, like a mixture of pitch and ashes, and ever since it has stayed with us in our history of the Magical West.

The following chapters present a series of expeditions into this great shadow, a shadow that once belonged to a single man. Each chapter was pulled from an ocean of possibilities. Countless churches that were dedicated to our magical saint, and his sister-in-spirit, Justina, must remain unnamed on these pages. Countless purported relics of the once-human body of our saint—such as the mummified arm in the seventeenth-century Zlătari Church in Bucharest—must go unexplored. And all the people who for many centuries have worked within his shadow will remain anonymous.

But they will be with us in spirit as we work our way back to the mythical man who once stood between the early Christian church and the sun of the ancient mystery cults, his shadow a bridge which lets us cross over to our pagan past. As with any journey made in darkness, we shall require particular tools for navigation: patience, trust, and a way to discern the path ahead that does not rely on the sight of our eyes. So before we set out on our expedition, a warning must be given about the nature of the territory to be explored.

In his masterpiece *Geosophia: The Argo of Magic*, Jake Stratton Kent reintroduced *mythical landscapes* to the modern reader, and in particular to the active student of Western magic and mysticism. A mythical landscape tends to blur with the physical land under our feet, yet it always remains distinct from it. Were we to stand in the ruins of an Egyptian temple, it would certainly be easier to blur the boundary between Egypt's physical and mythical topography and access the mythical stories and forces formed there long ago. But it is by no means necessary to travel physically to Egypt to access those forces and myths.

For a visionary magician, any place they stand, any place they breathe, can become a door. Where this door leads depends as much on the surrounding land's current qualities as on their ability to reach beyond these and connect with the mythical topography through which they wish to travel in spirit. It is true that not every mythical access point can be forced open from everywhere. Yet most mythical places can be extensively explored without any physical proximity.

It is this latter feature of the mythical world that we'll leverage extensively in the following chapters. As we read this book our bodies may rest in buses, tubes, or trains, on sofas, deck chairs or beds; yet our spirit will be free to travel through very different terrain. And the landscape we'll explore is more one of mythic memory than of mundane reality.

Unless we become adept magicians, our knowledge of the ancient Greek and Egyptian mystery cults' actual practices will always be highly limited, as it depends on a few remaining historical artefacts. Yet a careful study of these artefacts lets us learn a lot about how these cults have been remembered—and thus preserved, at least in their shadow-forms—over the centuries by our ancestors. These memories may not fully match the places and practices of their origins, yet for centuries they have been used as blueprints and ideals to shape new experiences and new generations. They are both myth and mundane reality, both shadow and flesh.

Such historic uncertainties and ambiguities should by no means discourage further exploration. The power of mythic patterns, whether they emerge fully-formed from a storyteller's vision or are bound together from multiple actual events, lies first and foremost in the sense-making mechanism they provide for the communities from which they emerge. The ability of myth to preserve, stabilize, and keep alive this sense-making mechanism over millennia is unparalleled—and the story of our mythical saint Cyprian is a powerful example of this. A myth never turns brittle for as long as its pattern is brought to life in the flesh of those confronted with it. Listening alone is not enough. Travelling within the story is what is required.

Without myths that shine a light on our own and our people's future, we can certainly keep on walking. But it would be a path without meaning, and with little promise to our own future selves.

The blind giant Orion carries his servant Cedalion on his shoulders to act as the giant's eyes. (Manuscript of allegorical and medical drawings, Library of Congress, Rosenwald 4, Bl. 5r)

Introduction

A body made from earth and light

> We are like dwarfs on the shoulders of giants, so that we can see more than they, and things at a greater distance, not by virtue of any sharpness of sight on our part, or any physical distinction, but because we are carried high and raised up by their giant size.
>
> — Bernard of Chartres

In the early twelfth century the philosopher Bernard of Chartres was first to use the metaphor that we are nothing but "dwarfs standing on the shoulders of giants."

Bernard was strongly influenced by Platonism and developed several of those ancient Greek concepts in his work. According to Bernard's natural philosophy, an intermediary medium exists between the realm of Platonic ideas and our material realm. These *formae nativae* or "forms of emergence" are living effigies of Plato's eternal ideas. Without these, the eternal ideas could not affect the physical world. The active agency of the *formae nativae* is essential for the cosmos to come into creation and to maintain its fertile powers. They are the living bridge between the eternal (or spiritual) and the ephemeral (or physical) realm.

According to Chartres, the *formae nativae* bring about the creation of all concrete, individual objects and lend them their species-specific properties—beginning with the four elements. In this manner they gild and beautify the entire previously formless universe. According to Bernard, even the human soul consists of such *formae nativae*.

As far as our exploration of the many faces of Cyprian of Antioch is concerned, Bernard's proverb is of twofold significance.

INTRODUCTION

Certainly, as Western magicians Cyprian of Antioch is one of the giants on whose shoulders we firmly stand. Many of the recent publications about him have looked at his historical significance, and how anonymous works of both folk and high magic have became associated with him over the seventeen centuries since the emergence of his and Justina's legend. In this respect his name has become a dark light, a kind of mystical compass that guides the aspirant's journey deeper and deeper into the chthonic caves of our magical tradition. Jake Stratton-Kent's massive two-volume work *The Testament of Cyprian the Mage* is the best and most complete illustration of where such a journey can lead us, and how many archaic forms and practices of our craft it can help us rediscover in a new light.

Yet there also is a second aspect—a more occult one, if you want—to Bernard's saying. For Cyprian the Mage is "a giant on whose shoulders we stand" not only in an historic sense, but also in a much more practical one.

What if 'Cyprian' was not only a tag that our ancestors used to classify and file certain works of magic under a specific banner? What if he was a living, breathing magical spirit in his own right? It's here that Bernard's idea of the *formae nativae* assumes a very practical relevance. As practising magicians, we depend on doorways between the material and spiritual realms. Witches and shamans of all ages and cultures have always relied on spirit relationships to form intermediary interfaces into the currents of power and divine forces with which humans are not meant to interfere.

It is in this practical sense that Cyprian of Antioch is so much more than a legendary saint who was banned from the Catholic Church's records. As we will discover, he is an actual emergent form in his own right, a living gateway into our own magical past, present, and possible future.

INTRODUCTION

Of course many such doorways or spirit intermediaries exist. Today magicians have an endless choice of spiritual allies and affiliations. Just as over recent decades our social network has gone from being tightly knit and durable to being much more fluid and interchangeable, so our spirit relationships seem to have evolved. Few magicians today seem to work with the same spirits for decades or lifetimes. The call of other, seemingly more exotic possibilities seems to become too loud and alluring to stay committed to longer-lasting relationships—whether this is with spirits or humans.

In the end, it's only fair to wonder why our magical relationships should be any different from our physical ones. For better or worse, it seems that marriages spanning a lifetime have seen the same decline as similar spirit relationships. Freedom seems to eat commitment for breakfast in all walks of life these days.

In light of the ocean of choice by which we are surrounded, let's be clear about what characterizes Cyprian of Antioch as a *formae nativae*. What is unique about him as a giant on whose shoulder we might choose to place our own magical practice?

What is unique about Cyprian as a spiritual being, compared to other forms of demons, angels, or divine associates, is that his body is essentially composite in nature. His (spirit) hands are not pure, but stained. The body of Cyprian of Antioch is made from both flesh and fire.

> Psellus was the bridge between Neo-Platonic, Gnostic and Hermetic texts and the theology, philosophy and demonology of the late Byzantine era: a bridge between the classical view of the daemon as a beneficial guiding spiritual presence, and the later Christian view of demons as intrinsically evil fallen angels.
>
> —Skinner, 2010

INTRODUCTION

To understand the relevance of our ancestor's compound body, let's open a book from the library of our magical past. Michael Psellus, in his treatise *On the Operation of Daemons*, has the following to say about the bodies of angels and daemons:

> The daemon tribe have a body, and are conversant with corporeal beings. And the divine Basilius maintains it, that not merely daemons but even the pure angels have bodies, being a sort of thin, aerial, and pure spirits; and in proof of this he adduces the testimony of David, most celebrated of the prophets, saying, 'He taketh his angels and spirits, and his messengers a flame of fire.' (...) but nothing can interpose opposition to an angel, because they present opposition to nothing, not being homogeneous with any thing; on the other hand, the bodies of daemons, thought constituted indistinct

by their tenuity, are yet in some measure material and palpable.

— Psellus, pp.61–62

The compound nature of Cyprian's body is daemonic in its purest sense: It is material and palpable, as Cyprian was once a human being. And yet it is also aerial, made of light and fire, as in his current form he is residing in the spirit realm. Like all saints in the vast corpus of the Catholic Church, but unlike most of the classical Western tradition's daemons and angels, Cyprian is thus a bridge between two seemingly separate worlds. He is a *formae nativae*, a mediating principle that, once we connect with it, permits us to travel back and forth between the many realms for which his compound body forms a gateway.

Cyprian of Antioch thus does not stand at the crossroads; his spiritual body *is* the crossroads.

This crossroads is multilayered and allows us to experience the many significant polarities of our magical path. In the focal point of Cyprian's body, we find ourselves confronted with the essential polarities that uphold the current, or *kinetic field*, of our spiritual practice.

As we shall explore in the following chapters, amongst the many polarities embodied by the myth of Cyprian of Antioch, the following five particularly stand out:

Polarities in the Myth of Cyprian of Antioch

the real world	*and*	*the mythic world*
the realm of flesh	*and*	*the realm of spirits*
the individual being	*and*	*the ancestral hive*
our angelic nature	*and*	*our demonic nature*
our moral deeds	*and*	*our immoral needs*

Cyprian as depicted in the confessio under the Saints John and Paul Basilica al Celio.

Chapter One

Cyprian the Ancient

a grave of dust or bones?

Whenever my studies have led me into this field, I have been particularly interested in the question of whether it is possible to distinguish between those cases where a specific person has initiated some sort of tradition which has then been embellished and expanded upon by other authors, and those cases where poetic fantasy has ruled freely over randomly-chosen names, and where no actual person, but a novella, formed the 'prius.'

— Reitzenstein, *Cyprian der Magier*, p.38

> The legend of Justina belongs to those cases that must be considered pure fiction.
> — Radermacher, *Griechische Quellen zur Faustsage*, p.5

At least since Richard August Reitzenstein's 1917 publication of *Cyprian der Magier* in *den Nachrichten von der Königlichen Gesellschaft der Wissenschaften zu Göttingen*, Cyprian, former mage and later saint, has widely been regarded as merely a legendary figure. In his philological study, Reitzenstein explained in great detail how the legend of Justina and Cyprian of Antioch was a prime example of a tradition founded mainly on literary creativity rather than historical accuracy. In his opinion, there was conclusive philological proof that the legend was simply a poetic fantasy built on familiar names and oral traditions of the time, which had given rise to a "certain kind of tradition." In a short note, *Zu Cyprian dem Magier*, published three

CHAPTER 1. CYPRIAN THE ANCIENT

years later in the *Archiv für Religionswissenschaft*, Reitzenstein assumed an even more definite and resolute tone, as if to drown out any remaining dissenting voices:

> I have given proof in (..., the previously mentioned article) that the veneration of Saint Cyprian of Antioch was built entirely upon a novella about a female ascetic, Justa (Justina), which itself was written for edification purposes around A.D. 350. (...) The hunt for the remains of a tradition in this delicate novella must now cease.
>
> — Reitzenstein, *Zu Cyprian dem Magier*, pp.236–237

Reitzenstein's academic assertiveness is interesting in itself, as he admittedly relied heavily on Theodor Zahn's 1882 German work, *Cyprian von Antiochien und die deutsche Faustsage*, in which Zahn reconstructed the original Greek text of the saint's first book from its many surviving fragments. (This work quickly became the basis for later translations of this text, even outside German-speaking countries.) Zahn, though, was much more careful than Reitzenstein in assessing the polarity between the mythical and historical realities encountered in our mage's tale:

> What has been said about 'Cyprianus' makes it very likely that one of the many goëts who populated Antioch from the first to the fourth century actually bore this name. (...) So could the tale be based on an ancient historical record? If this is the case, then admittedly such a record has by now been completely overgrown by much more recent ideas about, and versions of, the story.
>
> — Zahn, pp.108–109

CHAPTER 1. CYPRIAN THE ANCIENT

Unlike the stories of the sixteenth-century Dr. Faust, the magical lore surrounding St. Cyprian and Justina has always overshadowed the few remaining facts that point to their once having been real people. These facts, while they are few in number and cannot give us the whole, final truth behind the story of St. Cyprian, should not be overlooked or forgotten, as they unfortunately have been in many recent publications.

From Antioch to Rome

a secret ritual chamber

Why then the continuing discussion about the historical authenticity of the two saints, when their veneration was widely spread in both East and West, supported by writings documenting their *vita* and passion story, by the existence of a *sepulchrum Iustinae* in Antioch according to *Itinerarium Antonini Placentini*, the early medieval narrative of some Italians' pilgrimage to Minor Asia, and by the story of the relics brought from Rome to Piacenza?

— Jensen, *The Story of Justina and Cyprian of Antioch as told in a Medieval Lectionary from Piacenza*, p.10

The literary tradition of Cyprian and Justina is based on three different texts by three different authors. All three texts are usually dated to around A.D. 350. The first text, *Conversio Cypriani*, tells of Cyprian's conversion to Christianity and is mainly focused on Justina and the immense spiritual powers granted her for her strict piety. The second text, *Confessio Cypriani*, centres on St. Cyprian's repentance. It begins with the mage himself speaking in the first person, before going on to give an account of his tale. The third text, *Passio Cypriani*, focuses on the famous martyrdom that both Cyprian and Justina suffered, which is not mentioned in the other two texts.

Around the middle of the fifth century, the Roman Empress Aelia Eudocia (401–460 B.C.), who was the wife of Theodosius II (401–450 B.C.), brought together these three accounts, had them translated into a metric paraphrase, and published them in three books. Large parts of the first two books are still extant; we also have an abstract of all three books dating from the ninth century A.D..

Based on the vast archive of subsequent retellings of the legend it is possible to reconstruct the original text of the first book; unfortunately we no longer have access to the full original texts of the second and third books, but only to later versions of them (Jensen, pp.10–11, Wimmer, pp.198–199, Zahn, pp.15–20).

With the age of our source texts and their fragmentary state firmly in mind, we shall now attempt to mount a defence against Reitzenstein's firm position that Cyprian of Antioch was a myth from the very beginning, and argue that he was in fact once a mortal man.

And where better to start than by trying to locate his mortal remains? The last paragraph of the *Passio Cypriani* provides us with a clue as to what may have happened to them. Fragments of this text survive in Greek, Latin, Syrian, and Arabic versions, many of which were, starting from the beginning of the twentieth century, translated into German and published (Ryssel, p.273).

The most famous version of the *Passio Cypriani* is the Latin one titled *Acta SS. Cypriani & Justinae Martyrum*, published in the third volume of the massive *Thesaurus Novus Anecdotorum* in 1717. This text in fact contains a Latin version of all three books, and the *Passio Cypriani* is covered on four densely-printed pages titled *Passio SS. Cypriani et Justinae Virginis* (Martène, Durand, pp.1645–1650).

ACTA
SS. CYPRIANI ET JUSTINÆ
MARTYRUM.

The title of Acta SS. Cypriani & Justinae Martyrum.

However, a different version of this text was made accessible to a broader audience in 2012, when Brian Møller Jensen, from the University of Stockholm, published a bilingual, twelfth-century Italian liturgy dedicated to the life and death of Justina and Cyprian, in *The Story of Justina and Cyprian of Antioch as told in a Medieval Lectionary from Piacenza*. This liturgy is of extraordinary interest to our study, and not only because it is four hundred years older than the 1717 print of the *Acta* and formed part of a canon of writings that in its time was acknowledged by the Catholic Church.

This liturgy, which was read to the public in the Italian town of Piacenza as part of the religious festivities leading up to the Natale (feast day) of Justina of Antioch, is prime evidence of how the journey of our saint's relics was remembered up to the twelfth century:

> *Consummaverunt autem in Domino martyrium Cyprianus, Iustina et Theognitus. Fervius vero iussit corpora eorum canibus proici. Iacuerunt vero corpora diebus sex, et non tetigerunt ea ullae bestiae. Nautae vero fideles ex provincia Theogniti nocte venientes, cum dormirent, sanctorum corpora furati sunt. Elevaverunt in navem onus preciosum super aurum multum et navigaverunt de Nicomedia ad Romanam urbem, ferentes reliquias Cypriani et Iustinae virginis et Theogniti martyrum, attuleruntque preciosa munera Romae.*

CHAPTER 1. CYPRIAN THE ANCIENT

Suscepit autem haec sancta corpora Rufina, religiosa urbis matrona de genere claro. In quo loco demoniaci curantur, et variae infirmitates accipiunt sanitatem eorum meritis, glorificantes Patrem et Filium et Spiritum sanctum in secula seculorum. Amen.

— Jensen, pp. 88

Cyprian, Justina and Theognitus perfected their martyrdom in the Lord. Fervius ordered their bodies to be cast to the dogs. The corpses lay there for six days, and no beast touched them. Some faithful sailors from the same province as Theognitus came in the night, when the guards were sleeping, and stole the corpses of the saints. They lifted on board their ship a cargo more precious than much gold, and they sailed from Nicomedia to the city of Rome. Bringing the relics of the martyrs Cyprian, the virgin Justina and Theognitus, they brought precious gifts to Rome. The holy corpses were received by Rufina, a religious matron in the city and of noble descent. In that place people with evil spirits were cured, and people who were sick with various weaknesses received sanity through their merits, and they praised the Father, the Son and the Holy Spirit in all eternity. Amen.

— Jensen, p.89

But for the Arabic version, which omits this last paragraph of the third book altogether (Ryssel, pp. 311), all versions of the *Passio Cypriani* agree that the lady who received the saints' relics in Rome was a woman of noble descent called Rufina. They also all agree that she buried the three holy bodies in Rome.

But what else can we learn about the place where the remains were buried?

CHAPTER 1. CYPRIAN THE ANCIENT

In the Latin text of the *Acta* it is called a *loco laudabilis* (Martène, Durand, p.1649), which Zahn translates as "an extraordinary place." Though both the *Acta* and the twelfth-century liturgy are quite explicit about what made this place so extraordinary, Zahn limits himself to saying, euphemistically, that it was somewhere "where all kinds of sufferings were healed." (Zahn, pp.72). The Piacenza liturgy, on the other hand, directly states that it was a place where people were healed from daemonic possession—*demoniaci curantur*—as does the Latin *Acta*:

> *In quo loco nunc omnes qui daemonia habent & varias infirmitates, accipiunt sanitatem (...)*
>
> — Martène, Durand, pp.1649

> In this place, now, everyone who had demons and various diseases welcomed health again (...)
>
> — tr. Frater Acher

Cyprian of Antioch is widely known as a patron saint of magicians (e.g. ConjureMan Ali., *Saint Cyprian: Saint of Necromancers*, Hadean Press, 2011). Much of this is due to his having been a pagan mage before his conversion to Christianity. What is less well-known today, however, is how Cyprian's magic continued *after* his conversion.

To my knowledge, the above quotes from the *Acta* and the Piacenza liturgy are the earliest examples of the post-conversion continuity of Cyprian's magic. Here, in the Catholic Church's own records, the relics of Justina and Cyprian of Antioch are described as the newly embedded heart of a sacred place dedicated to curing daemonic possession and related bodily ailments.

After this, as far as most sources are concerned, no more specific details are given as to the location of our saints' relics: the legend holds that they were buried in an unknown sacred place in Rome in the fourth century. Most academics, following

Chapter 1. Cyprian the Ancient

Reitzenstein's 1917 and 1920 assessments, consider this a sufficiently vague and unspecific end—like the whole tale—not to merit further investigation.

Luckily for us, the Italian scholar Pio Franchi di Cavallieri was an exception to that rule. In 1935 he published an almost entirely forgotten article titled *Where have they been buried, Saint Cyprian, Justina, and Theoctist?* (Cavallieri, *Dove furono sepolti i SS. Cipriano, Giustina e Teoctisto?*, in: Note Agiogra-fiche, 8 (Studi e Testi 65), Rome 1935, §335–354). Through careful research, Cavallieri managed to uncover not only the place "where evil spirits were cured" but also the possible tomb of our two saints.

Cavallieri was the first scholar to examine a small underground shrine in a Roman church which had been excavated in the late nineteenth century and relate it to our magical saint. The church in question is the Saints John and Paul Basilica al Celio, which famously was built on top of an existing house in the

The entrance to the confessio below the Saints John and Paul Basilica al Celio.

fourth century. This church is also referred to as Santi Giovanni e Paolo al Celio and SS Giovanni e Paolo.

In 1887, while searching for the tombs of the martyrs John and Paul (not to be confused with the apostles!), several large underground sites were discovered below the basilica. During the following excavations twenty decorated rooms were discovered belonging to at least five different buildings which dated between the first and fourth centuries A.D.. These five buildings comprise one of the best preserved Roman residential building complexes still in existence today, and one of the best examples of a *domus ecclesiae*, or "house church."

One of those fourth-century underground rooms was a *confessio*, a shrine for personal prayer and ritual, dedicated to St. Cyprian and Justina. From an inscription on the wall, Cavallieri was able to learn more about the background of the shrine: it had been built by a Roman noblewoman called Rufina.

And this *confessio* matched the records of Empress Eudocia in ways other than just its owner's name being Rufina: the Greek version of Eudocia's text states that the remains of Cyprian and Justina lie in Rome "in a temple of the Divine Claudius, on top of the Caelian Hill." (Cavallieri, p.338)

The church, which nowadays is underground, though it was at street level in the fourth century, can still be visited today. There, through a hole in the wall of the shrine, one can still see the three graves where the remains of the martyrs were allegedly buried.

Now, private churches within the city boundaries of ancient Rome were extremely rare, and the burial of mortal remains outside of certain dedicated zones wasn't normally allowed:

> It (...) represents an early instance of a saintly body translated to a domus ecclesiae inside the city, the first such occurrence known from Rome. The very

Chapter 1. Cyprian the Ancient

novelty of a burial inside the city indicates the supramundane status of these saints. The special and separate cult space in effect specifically argues that the recipient was worthy of a cult, and the images assist in fixing this idea. The confessio is ornamented with the earliest preserved representations of hagiographic narrative.

— Cynthia Hahn, *Seeing and Believing*, 1997, p.1093

Given the unique and private nature of this ancient church, it's likely a formal cult for the three buried saints was never established. Instead it is likely that Pammachius, the founder of the basilica, built his much larger church on top of Cyprian and Justina's shrine at a time when their history had been forgotten. Nevertheless, the building of this basilica successfully maintained their resting place as a holy site down to the present day.

The frescoes in the cramped confessio under the Basilica SS Giovanni e Paolo.

Chapter 1. Cyprian the Ancient

The confessio underneath the church of SS Giovanni e Paolo, however, holds another critical hint about the magical nature of St. Cyprian. As is so often the case in magic, this clue is so obvious that it is easy to overlook.

On entering the cramped confessio, one is surrounded by a series of ancient frescos representing aspects of the stories of St. Cyprian, Justina, and Theoctist (Theognitus). Right in the middle of the richly ornamented space, and directly underneath the opening that leads to the three burial places, is the image of a standing man. He is dressed in traditional Roman clothes, his arms and hands are wide open in the classic iconographical pose of benediction, and he appears from behind two pulled-back veils. To his left and right, two figures kneel in adoration and prayer.

The central image of this nameless saint, right in front of the possible tomb of St Cyprian and Justina, does not gaze heavenwards. Rather, in the style of the Coptic icons which reflect Egyptian and Hellenistic influence, he looks directly at us in a forward gaze, greeting any visitors who enter this space to perform their ritual prayer and vision.

This image cannot be intended merely as adornment. The confessio is too small for there to be any space free for pure decoration. Instead this central feature must have a specific function, one related to the ritual activity for which this space was consecrated, and for which it was maintained for centuries.

This (possible) fresco of Cyprian as a young man, during his time as a pagan mage, is an interface to be worked with in vision. The drawn-back veils, behind which he appears, are an obvious clue to this function, as are the people praying to his sides and the directness of his gaze at whomever has come to work with him in prayer.

The fresco, open to the public every day, might be one of the earliest surviving Christian images to illustrate the actual function of saints in ritual and visionary magic. The key is right in front of us; we have only to open our eyes to see it. Saints (or spiritual ancestors, in other traditions) are magical interfaces. Half-human, half-spirit, they have become visionary doors that can be worked with to perform magical acts by engaging their mediation on the 'other side.' Now, obviously a mere image on a wall is no substitute for the magical act of working with a saint in vision. However, as it is a charged image created by an artist or artists mediating Cyprian's presence, it can function as an excellent bridge for a magical practitioner with the necessary visionary technique to engage with it.

Surprisingly, this ancient clue to the magical function of our magical saint was deciphered not by another mage, but by Cynthia Hahn, Professor of Art History at Hunter College, in her previously quoted article *Seeing and Believing*. In this article on ancient iconography, published in 1997, she perfectly describes the technical, magical function of this unique image:

Thus it is perhaps not surprising that the central figure of the SS. Giovanni e Paolo icon has certain qualities of a vision. He (...) becomes the earliest surviving instance of an icon image substituting for the devotee's personal vision of a saint in a shrine. Most remarkable is the clarity of the function of the saint in the icon. He is remote and otherworldly; he is to be venerated; and he prays in the orant pose of the catacombs. However, his eyes are not lifted to heaven but are directed out to the viewer. The icon is less a unique portrait of an individual saint than an object lesson in the function of a saint as intercessor.

— Hahn, 1997, p.1094f

CHAPTER 1. CYPRIAN THE ANCIENT

Via Piacenza to Milan

the urn of St. Cyprian

After their installation in the private *confessio* in Rome, the story of our saint's relics is as quiet as the grave for the several centuries during which his and Justina's remains remained untouched below the basilica in Rome.

Then, almost five hundred years later, we find a note that describes their *translatio*—the official relocation of their relics from Rome to Piacenza—in the year 1001. This note is preserved in the above-mentioned twelfth-century liturgical manuscript titled *Liber Magistri*:

> *Translatio beatae Iustinae virginis et martyris a Roma in Placentiam, cuius corpus una cum martyre Cypriano tradidit Sigefredo episcopo venerabilis papa Iohannes, qui huius civitatis antea fuit antistes.*
>
> — Jensen, p.5

The translation of the beautiful virgin and martyr Justina from Rome to Piacenza, whose body was delivered, together with the one of the martyr Cyprian, to Siegfried, the venerable bishop under Pope Johannis, who was the bishop in this city before.

— tr. Frater Acher

Siegfried of Piacenza (997–1031) was a German Benedictine bishop and the worldly ruler of the powerful northern Italian city of Piacenza. According to this note, the remains of both Justina and St. Cyprian of Antioch were officially "translated" to his city, where they were initially placed in a church next to the duomo due to heavy ongoing construction work. While one might question the trustworthiness of this single source, we do in fact see a widespread cult of Justina emerging across the Lombardy region from the turn of the first millennium (Sigrid Popp, pp.99–100).

CHAPTER 1. CYPRIAN THE ANCIENT

Some sources state that the remains of Justina and St. Cyprian were kept in the cathedral of Piacenza until the mid-sixteenth century, while others claim that their remains are there to this day. Still others insist that their remains were moved from the St. Lawrence Cemetery in Rome to Lisbon, Portugal in 1777, where they were placed in the Church of St. Anthony.

Whichever version you believe, to this day the virgin martyr Justina of Antioch is still the patron saint of the city of Piacenza, as could be dramatically witnessed during the millennial anniversary, in 2001, of the translation of her and St. Cyprian's relics to Piacenza:

> (...) on the feast day the bishop invited the congregation to the cathedral to attend the performance of a modern Gesamtkunstwerk that made use of liturgical, poetical, musical, dramatic and artistic elements to present the life and

passion story of Justina and Cyprian and ended in the crypt in front of the shrine containing their relics (...)

— Jensen, p.6

For the living cult of our saints, it matters little that the actual urn in which parts of their relics were kept for centuries was rediscovered in the early 1970s some forty miles away from their claimed resting places in the ritual crypt underneath the dome of Piacenza. Nor does it seem to matter that, on investigation, this reliquary casket unfortunately turned out to be empty.

Empty or not, we can still marvel at the artefact itself, which was crafted in Lombardy in the eleventh century, slightly after the translation of our saint's relics to Piacenza.

The precious reliquary casket is made from walnut and decorated by eight chiselled, partially gilded silver plates. It is a remarkable example of what medieval goldsmiths could achieve. Since its rediscovery in the 1930s, multiple scholars have confirmed its "indisputable authenticity," and have consistently considered it a very rare example of religious craftsmanship in the Lombardy region (Tasso, p.125).

On its eight richly decorated plates we find not only a detailed image of St. Cyprian and Justina's martyrdom, but also an image of the above-mentioned Siegfried of Piacenza, as well as a symbolic representation of the translation of their relics to Piacenza.

> The reliquary is connected with the translation of Saint Giustina's relics from Rome to Piacenza, carried out in 1001 by the antipope Johannes Philagathus, with the support of the bishop of Piacenza Sigifried; the bishop is probably represented among four saints, in one of the scenes on the slanting top of

The reliquary casket

Chapter 1. Cyprian the Ancient

The reliquary casket, other side

Figure 1.1: Detail of the martyrdom of Cyprian and Justina from the reliquary casket

> the casket. Moreover, the date of the translation is perfectly compatible with the dating proposed (...)
>
> — Tasso, p.136

Francesca Tasso, in her recent examination of this artefact—which now is on public display

Chapter 1. Cyprian the Ancient

Journey of St. Cyprian and Justina's mortal remains, legendary or real, from Nicomedia to Rome to Piacenza.

in the museum of the Castello Sforzesco in Milan—concluded that the urn was crafted specifically to hold parts of the saints' relics, particularly Justina's, so that they could be transported more easily during the religious parade and festivities that took place each year on September 26th.

Conclusion

In this first chapter we set out to explore aspects of St. Cyprian's role as a mediator between the real and the legendary worlds. Our search followed the traces left by the relics of Justina and Cyprian in our Western religious history. We followed their journey from fourth-century Asia Minor to a secret ritual crypt in Rome, all the way to the Cathedral of Our Lady in Piacenza, and to the lost reliquary casket of St. Cyprian which is now on display in a Milanese castle.

Standing at the crossroads, we always get to choose our path and perspective. We may well choose to understand each milestone of these relics' journeys as proof for the once-physical reality of their owners. But it is worth remembering that powerful agendas, political and religious, shaped and marked the narratives of our past just as much as they do those of our present.

Chapter 1. Cyprian the Ancient

Did Christian sailors truly pick up our saints' bodies from a beach? Were their relics really buried in a Roman crypt? And were parts of these relics ultimately translated to Piacenza (and possibly later to Lisbon), where for centuries people believed that their mortal remains rested in a wooden casket? For now these questions must remain a matter of faith, not fact. Looking at the remaining facts alone, we cannot come to a conclusion either way. We can say neither that Cyprian of Antioch once lived in the flesh, nor that he did not.

But from the evidence presented, we can conclude that recent books and studies, rather than doing their own research, have relied mainly on Reitzenstein's assessments, which were published in 1917 and 1920. These assessments were based purely on surviving written records: Reitzenstein was a philologist, not an historian or an archaeologist. And despite his brilliance as a philologist, we must take issue with his opinion that Cyprian of Antioch was nothing more than a mythical figure woven out of scraps of previous tales and names. The philological evidence available to him in the early twentieth century may indeed have pointed strongly in that direction; however, the historical and textual evidence that has since come to light clearly suggests that a reassessment is in order.

Just as stories create perceived realities, so the realities of our past disappear behind the stories of our present. The body of St. Cyprian could not be a better metaphor for this powerful dynamic. Stepping back from his legend and lore, we can truly see him in his hybrid nature: half born from human flesh, half woven from timeless myth.

Chapter Two

Cyprian of Two Worlds

a priest of good or evil?

The Oratio Cypriani

blessing the lineage

Beside the three books recounting Justina and Cyprian's legend, there is another document from the fourth century A.D. that has to do with our mage. This is the *Oratio Cypriani* or "Prayer of Cyprianus," which has been preserved in Greek, Arabic, and Ethiopian versions. The textual history of this prayer begins with the Greek original, which was composed in the fourth century. It then moves on to its Arabic translation, and finally assumes its most recent form in Ethiopian.

In 1903 the German professor of patrology Theodor Schermann offered the first reconstruction of the original Greek text, making use of the six surviving Greek manuscripts known at the time which were held in various European libraries. None of these documents were actually younger than the fourteenth century. However Schermann, following Karl Michel, who had published on the *Oratio Cypriani* only one year previously, was able to date the original source document back to the fourth century A.D., from which he assumed his versions had been copied and further evolved. Thus both scholars assumed they were working with pseudo-Cyprianic documents which derived from an original version most likely penned, in their opinion, in the fourth century A.D. by Cyprian of Antioch himself.

> (Michel) assumed that the Latin Prayers of Cyprianus as well as an Arabic version

> could be traced back to a Greek original which emerged around the year 400 A.D.. The pagan sorcerer Kyprianos of Antioch who converted to Christianity has to be assumed as the presumable originator. (...) The Prayers of Cyprianus suffered the same fate as the related legend of Cyprianus which is no longer available in its original form but only in later revisions.
>
> — Schermann, pp.305–306

Michel and Schermann's central argument for dating the original versions of the *Oratio Cypriani* to the fourth century A.D. is based on the long sequences of saints and church fathers that the text calls upon. As random as these sequences might seem to the modern reader, names listed in a particular order were a central aspect of early Christian liturgy. Through the help of other documents whose origin can be dated without doubt, unique traditions bound to specific locations and times can be identified.

In particular Schermann leverages for comparison a *kontaktion* contained in *Cod. Vatic. 2282*, a hymn performed in the Orthodox Church and Eastern Catholic Churches that follow the Byzantine Rite. This hymn, which originates from the Patriarchy of Antioch (Damascus), contains list of sacred names that exactly matches the *Oratio Cypriani* in both structure and sequence.

> The Prayers (of Cyprianus) in this case prove to be even more original and more precisely local than the liturgy (...). In any case such circumstance supports that Antioch was the prayers' homeland as well as their author's, who was already known to Gregor of Nazianz as the pagan sorcerer who later converted to Christianity, Cyprianus of Antioch.
>
> — Schermann, p.306

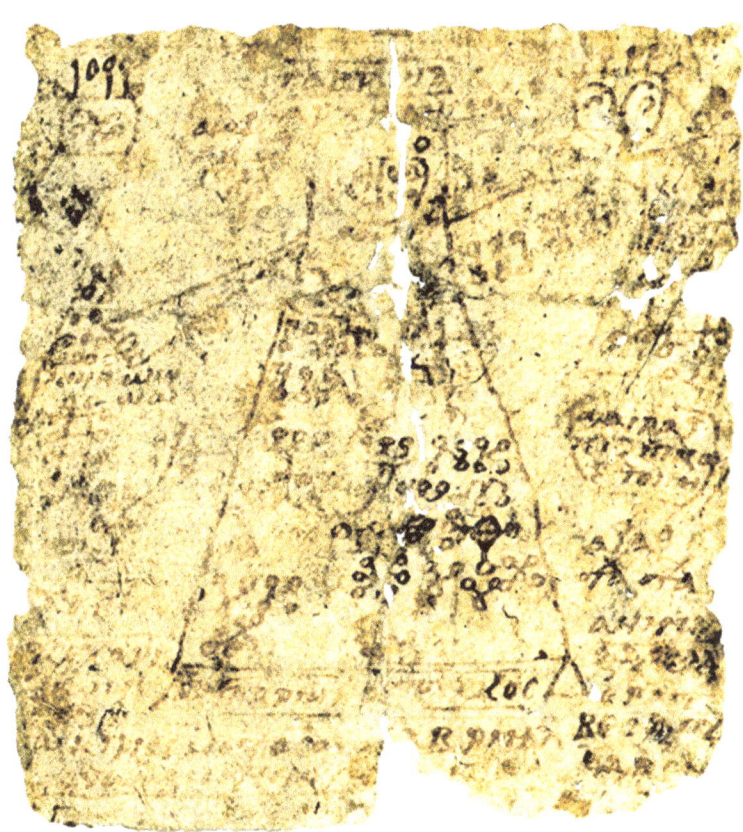

The angel Gabriel as he appears in the Ethiopian Grimoire of Cyprian (P. Heid. inv. Kopt. 684)

Towards the end of the First World War (1917–1918), Adolf Grohmann, the Austrian scholar of Arabic, Semitic, and Egyptian, was first to compare all then-known versions of this prayer, and to reconstruct a coherent original version of the Ethiopian prayer.

This chapter offers a full English translation of Grohmann's version of this ancient prayer. As we will see in our analysis of its various sections, it represents a curious compendium of the magical knowledge and practice of its time.

The Ancient Prayer of Cyprian

1. In the name of the Father and of the Son and of the Holy Spirit, of the one God! 2. Prayer of Cyprian (Kuaepreyanos), may his intercession be

with us, Amen. 3. This prayer is strength for the kings and expulsion for the Satans and for the evil eye and for the evil gaze, and (liberation for the captivated), and for the expulsion of evil dreams. 4. (Praise be to God in the heavens and peace on earth for the pleasure of man. 5. Praise be to God in the heavens and peace on earth for the pleasure of man. 6. Praise be to God in the heavens and peace on earth for the pleasure of man.) 7. And on the day of the Sabbath, which God sanctified and blessed, and upon which he thwarted every action of evil, I, Cyprianus, the servant to Jesus Christ elevated my wisdom and my thought to God, both prayed and demanded of him and said:

This first section serves as a general introduction to the ritual prayer. The second verse simply calls out the title with an added request for St. Cyprian's intercession. The third verse explains the general function of the ritual prayer. After the threefold request for God's blessing for the long prayer to come, the ritualist shifts their viewpoint and speaks from the perspective of Cyprian himself.

Assuming the identity and perspective of a divine being in ritual was a cornerstone of ancient (Egyptian) rituals. It served as an access point to the divine realm by letting go of the mortal identity of the ritualist and, as the prayer so eloquently explains, "elevated" their wisdom and thought to God. Having ritually assumed the form of Cyprian, one may speak as an equal among spirits and divine beings. It is from this viewpoint that demands can be uttered towards the long and expansive row of saints, martyrs, and apostles as we'll encounter them in this prayer.

> 8. You, O Lord, (Lord of the mighty), (Almighty), who holds together the universe, his throne is light, marvellous,

and holy; and praised you are from the beginning. 9. You know the deeds of your servant. 10. So I persisted in the works of the devil and while I did not know your name, I was one of them who bound the heavens so that rain would not come to the earth, and the earth so that it might not give its fruit, and the trees of the field so that they might not give their fruits. And as I walked past a herd of sheep, I usually made everything that was in their bowels come out, and similarly I bound pregnant woman so that they could not give birth, and I prevented the fishes of the ocean from going into the water or for it to beat its wave; and in the wealth of my malice and my sin all of this was within my power. 11. But now, my Lord and my God, I have known thy holy name, and love thy pure name, and have returned to thee and to thy commandment, O Mercy of Mercy; and I require you, and ask by your beloved only Son, the perfect and completed one, who does not wane (from his divine nature):

Verses 8 to 11 deepen the mystical shift in perspective and further help the ritualist identify with the viewpoint of the magical Saint. Here perspective is offered on his long and sinful past as well as his conversion to the Christian faith.

From a psychological point of view, this opening is extremely smart and impactful. By identifying with the extreme, devilish deeds of this Saint right at the start of the prayer, the ritualist's personal lapses and breaches will seem small and irrelevant. Thus, despite their own shortcomings, their confidence will be strengthened that indeed they hold the right to demand their being unbound from any spell or sorcery that has been put upon them.

Having complete faith in the efficacy of one's

own ritual action is a fundamental prerequisite for successful magical practice. This traditional shift in identity helps achieve precisely that: to overcome any doubts as to whether the practitioner themselves is worthy or powerful enough to perform the ritual successfully. Now they are no longer one with their mortal identity; now they have shifted into the identity of a saint, speaking to their own lineage of ancestors from the empowered vantage point of a genuine link in the spiritual chain.

> 12. The sky shall be opened and rain shall fall on the earth and the earth shall give of its fruit again; and also the trees on the fields shall give of their fruits again; and the barren women shall give perfect children and they shall suck milk from their mother. 13. Also the fishes in the sea, and everything that it contains, shall be unbound from where it was bound. 14. And unbound shall be the birds of

the sky and all animals of the earth and every man to whom was done evil, and every evil deed itself; 15. All this shall be unbound from every man, nor may it be bound through sorcery or a holy name; and all Satans shall flee before him and everything evil and impure cannot stand before me, I who prays this. 16. And may he turn void all sorcery and all evil, and purify his soul and his flesh and his wholeness; and may God make him strong against Satan and all his power, through your holy and prosperous name that is sanctified and praised in heaven and on earth.

Verses 12 to 16 highlight an essential aspect of this ancient prayer. Notably, in this first plea for being freed from spells and sorcery and the affliction of the evil Satans, no specific Christian references are made at all. Instead the ritualist turns first to earth and nature. By ensuring that the natural forces are "unbound" and can follow their natural patterns, the ritualist reestablishes the necessary foundations for success of any magical act to come. As highlighted in the Introduction, all magic that attempts to affect the world of creation has to work through nature as its *formae nativae*. As a result, if some previous magical spell had successfully bound out these generative forces from performing their natural work—or even merely crippled them somewhat—then no subsequent magical act could work before the previous restrictions had been undone.

Just like the legend of Justina and Cyprian, where pagan magic is overthrown by Christian magic, this prayer attempts to overthrow whatever kind of magic had previously been performed by calling for a magical "unbinding" which is to be performed by nature and spiritual saints working in conjunction. This is highlighted in verse 15 in particular, where

Cyprian makes plain that the following magical plea is directed against any act of magic, goëtic or holy.

> 17. And just as the rock opened and water burst forth, and just as the Children of Israel drank (thereof), just like that, O Lord, raise your hand, which is full of mercy over the soul and body of your servant. 18. And if he places this scripture in his house, so may the power of my God be with him, Amen.

Verse 17 introduces a narrative plot specific to the Old Testament. Identification with the people of Israel, however, will not remain exclusive. As we will see later on, the prayer will call on the gods of all monotheistic religions as well as pagan ones. What matters most in this general ritual for expulsion is to cast the net as widely as possible, even across the boundaries of spiritual currents where necessary, in order to gather all possible 'keys' that might unlock the bonds brought upon the ritualist.

Verse 18 is of particular note, as it helps us understand how this prayer was used in practice. As we'll see in later sections, our prayer is referred to several times as a "book" or "scripture" that the ritualist has "opened" or subsequently placed somewhere. Clearly the manuscript of the written prayer had a strongly talismanic function. As the prayer refers to the acts of "opening the book" and reading it aloud, and also placing the book within a space that is to be purified and positively affected by its powers, we have to assume that the book was used in both these ways.

It seems likely that the ritualist would have first created a dedicated copy of the entire prayer, then performed it out loud, and finally placed the manuscript in a designated place to keep up its magical effect. The manuscript Grohmann used for his restoration consisted of eighty-five small folio pages, filled with Ethiopian characters. We have to assume that versions of the original prayer were not only placed in houses or dwellings, but also written on continuous scrolls of animal skin, rolled up, sealed, and stored in an amulet container small enough to wear on one's body. Indeed, all these practices are still performed by today's Coptic Christians.

Furthermore, we have to assume that such work was not only done by magicians for magicians, but also offered as a service to clients. Just being able to write a scroll or manuscript of such length was a rare skill, and this act in itself was often perceived to have a magical effect. It was also an expensive undertaking, as either papyrus or animal skins had to be prepared or purchased to write on.

Here we are confronted with a general problem in assessing the genuineness of any magical act. From ancient times a central aspect of magic consisted of performing acts of *epiclesis*: calling to the gods and drawing down their divine forms into more ephemeral shapes which can be experienced through our subjective human lens. When the imprint of such an act was contained in a physical object—such as a statue, stone, wand, cup, altar, bread, or roll of scripture—then the magician priest had created a rare artefact that others would be willing to pay for. What better product to sell than the echo of a divine being captured in a physical object?

This polarity between a genuine magical act and the myriad opportunities for humans to exploit it financially requires any student of magic to be very careful when reading up on ancient magical practices. Without following the instructions and performing the magical act ourselves, we will never know whether we have the genuine notes of a real magician or merely an expensive marketing leaflet from an age before the printing press.

> 19. O Lord, as you have planted the Garden of Eden ('Edom) at the beginning of the days and as you created the rivers

Gihon (Giyon) and Phison ('Efeson), Tigris (Tegros) and Euphrates ('Afratos), that water the entire earth, that nobody can withstand or fight off, that is how Satan the evil and impure cannot affect anything. Be it a charm or the evil eye or evil sorcery, he cannot persist against this scripture which I have opened today. 20. And may it be far from your servant N.N. everything evil and impure, Amen.

The narrative plot of the Old Testament is now continued, leading into the earliest acts of creation. Again the eternal forces of nature are conjured to help the ritualist, here in the shape of the four original rivers, representing the living powers of the four cardinal directions.

In verse 20 we first encounter the actual name of the ritualist, or possibly that of their client. In Grohmann's original document the name was given as Viktor or Wiktor. It is doubtful that this was the actual name of either the client or the person performing the prayer: the name Viktor comes from the Latin verb *vincere*, "conquer," and so it simply means 'conqueror' or even 'winner.' It was a popular name among early Christians, and was borne by several saints and three popes. Given the meaning of the name, we should assume that it was used in this prayer as a placeholder which further emphasized the positive powers of the ritualist over the 'evil' forces they attempted to expel.

Thus it has been deliberately replaced in our English version by the traditional placeholder "N.N." (*nomen nescio*) to indicate an unknown person. Anybody who attempts to perform this prayer will need to insert their own given name in its place.

> 21. Expel therefore, O Lord, from your servant and from all men, (the ones) who stand against the world of the 72 languages; and tamed may be the Evil One and all his hosts and all his power

and all his work. Expel them from your servant and purify his soul and his flesh and his wholeness by the power of God and by the power of the 67 angels, who descended into the city of 'Akrelyos, and by the names of the cherubim and the seraphim, (who) sing hymns in front of the throne of the living God. 22. Through his name I unbound and unbind all sorcery and spell and every evil eye and all things bad, by the prayer of the angels, who are spread out in the world, and, may it be, by this unbinding (scroll) in this house, Amen, and the letting go of all evil doers, who do (it), (that are) evil men, Amen.

The "world of the 72 languages" is another Biblical reference. Early Christians knew seventy-two descendants of Noah's three sons Shem, Ham, and Japheth. According to the *Vocabularium*

CHAPTER 2. CYPRIAN OF TWO WORLDS

Aethiopicum, seventeen names (i.e. biblical characters whose later lineages founded nations or ethnicities) derived from Shem, thirty from Cham, and twenty-five from Japheth. Thus this traditional ethnology represents the expansion of humankind from the descendants of Noah and their dispersion into many lands after the Flood. The "Evil One," therefore, is meant as the spiritual power that resists such a natural expansion of mankind from the original seed of Noah. The sixty-seven angels who descended into the city of Akrelyos is a reference whose source neither Grohmann nor any other scholar has been able clearly to identify.

> 23. I unbound and unbind through the name of God so that the impure Satan cannot bear up against me in any shape, whether at night or day; and may legions (Legeyon) be banned and all his power and all his hosts by the ban of St. Peter (Petros), the head of the Apostles. I

unbound and unbind from your servant any spell and bond, and every evil eye, by the prayer of the High, and by the intercession of the wakeful, and by the purity of the pure, and by the wandering of the wanderers, and by the creation of our father Adam ('Adam), and by the sacrifice of Abel ('Abel), and by the power of Seth (Set), and by the vision of Henoch (Henok), and by the pure Mary (Maryam), and by the solitude of David (Dawit), and by the sanctification of Henoch (Henok), and by the ban of Melchi(sedek) (Malki), and by the salvation of Noah (Noh), and by the birth of Sem (Sem), and by the faith of Abraham ('Abreham), and by the sacrifice of Isaac (Yeshak), whom he (God) made descend to be replaced by a ram and whom he saved from the butcher's knife; and by the priesthood of Melchisedeks (Malka Sedek), and by the prophecy of Jacob (Ya'kob), and by the beauty of Joseph (Yosef), and by the patience of Hiob ('Lyob), and by the captivation of Isaac (Yeshak), and by the love of Benjamin (Benyam), and by the power of Joshua ('Iyasu) the son of Nawe, and by the priesthood of Aaron (Aron), and by the prayer of Phinehas (Finahas), and by the psalms of David (Dawit), and by the tears of Elias ('Elsa'), and by the love of Jephtas (Yoftahe), and by the prophecy of Jessaia ('Isayyas), and by the mourning of Yeremiah ('Ermeyas), and by the murder of Zachariah (Zakaryas), and by the prophecy of the prophets, and by the sanctification of those who do not sleep, and by the purity of those who do not sin, and by the depths of the deep and the rolling of thunder, and by the drifting of the clouds and the might of the lightning flashes, and by the movement of the clouds and by the hierarchy of the angels, and by the commandments of the archangels, and by the vision of Moses (Muse), and by the sanctification of the Apostle, and by the birth of Jesus ('Iyasus), and by his baptism in the Jordan (Yordanos), and by the voice who called him, saying: "This one is my son whom I love, with whom I am well pleased; him you shall hear," and by him who changed water into wine, and by him who rebuked the sea, and by him who raised the son of the widow, and by him who raised Lazarus ('Al'azar) from the grave, and by him who calmed the sea at the feet of St. Peter (Petros), his servant, and by him who was crucified and buried and resurrected from the dead on the third day as is written, and who on his ascent into the heavens is amongst the splendour of the angels, and by the myriads of arch-priests who served him when he ascended to heaven, and by the blood, and by the intercession of the imprisoned, and by the hardship of the hermits, and by their faith which never was proven wrong: may there be dissolved from your servant N.N. every spell, and all envy, and every evil eye, and every act of wrongdoing, whether (these) were done in secrecy or in public, through the splendour of God, the creator of creation, by the word that was called out by Christ (Krestos) while he was crucified on the wood of the cross and said: ("Elohe, Elohe, Elohe, why have you abandoned me?"), and by the name of

God the mighty, the praised one: we want to pray to the Father, and the Son, and the Holy Spirit in all eternity, Amen.

Verses 23 as well as 32 stand out due to the length and breadth of the *dramatis personae* which they call on for support.

Verse 23 begins by clearly recapitulating the goal of the invocation: to ward off and expel any kind of evil from the person for whom the prayer is performed, whether in the shape of binding spells, sorcery, the evil eye, or direct demonic attacks. Then the prayer invokes a long Biblical lineage for support. It begins with the nameless "wakeful" and "wanderers" before it touches on Adam as the first of mankind. From here the full succession of Biblical descendants are invoked, only stopping with the prophet-priest Zechariah, the mythical father of John the Baptist, whose name literally means "remember God." Then a second call for the wakeful ones "who do not sleep" is inserted before the prayer turns to invoke the forces of nature to acquire their support as well.

The second part of the verse is dedicated to the invocation of Jesus as the figurehead of the New Testament. Some of his miraculous deeds are evoked, as well as his final ascension into heaven. Then the purpose of the prayer is repeated again, before the verse closes with a general commitment to pray "in all eternity" to the Father, Son, and Holy Spirit.

In his formidable article *Demon Invocations in the Coptic Magical Spells*, Boston University scholar David Frankfurter provides wonderful insights into the inner 'architecture' of ritual prayers such as this one. Frankfurter, who specializes in Jewish and Christian apocalyptic literature, magical texts, popular religion, and Egypt in the Late and Roman periods, clearly spots that by the time we reach the Coptic period of magic, many different traditions have already come together and the boundaries between them have become heavily blurred. In such a context—not too different from ours today, where very few magical practices still stem from a single 'pure' tradition, and most carry the marks of centuries of creative syncretism—the magician's role is at least twofold: equal parts composer and performer. The work of composing magical liturgy for performance is of particular pertinence to our analysis of the Prayer of Cyprian:

> Each spell represents, fundamentally, the creative, *ad hoc* constructions of tradition—the bricolages—of a ritual expert, probably a monk or church scribe. He composes the invocation, the gestures, and the ingredients to convey efficacy through the combined features of tradition—that these are ancient names and figures; authority—that these are recognizable names and figures associated with power, perhaps with the church and

its liturgical lore; and pertinence—that the words spoken, the substances used, the whole «theatre» of ritual binding, pertains intrinsically to the experience of the client. The whole process of collecting and editing master spells and presiding over their performance involves this kind of creative synthesis, in which the choice and articulation of spirits comprise the key component.

— Frankfurter, pp.6–7

While the focus of this work is not to make a spell but in fact the very opposite, its underlying construction still utilizes the same approach. All three key components—tradition, authority, and pertinence—have been perfectly combined into a single form in our prayer so far, specifically in verse 23.

It is critical to emphasize that terms such as "construction," "composer," or "performance" should not diminish our respect for the magical act encompassed in this prayer or in similar spells. Any magical act, however small or casual it may seem, is a performance in its original Latin sense: the achievement of something. Whether that achievement is genuine or spurious, authentic or fake, is always down to the individual performance. Of course the best way to assess the soundness of any magical construction is to perform it ourselves. Quickly we will learn how its components come together (or do not) to create the multilayered achievements that mark any deep ritual experience.

These are: (a) the induction of bodily ritual trance through the use of language, melody, and/or movement; (b) the creation of proper spiritual contact to one or more entities relating to the magical matter at hand; (c) the collaborative creation between both spiritual performers (spirit and man) to achieve a specific goal; (d) the subsequent physical, mental, and time-related echo of the spirit's presence within our body, mind, and life.

Unfortunately all the above criteria are of a deeply subjective nature. Thus any magic that is not performed in secrecy always faces the very real risk of turning into a performance in its negative sense, i.e. into public entertainment.

However, irrespective of this omnipresent risk, we have to accept that any magical act is a construct, and thus a cultural artefact. Like the hybrid character of our St. Cyprian, every act of magic is a crossbreed, the offspring of a communion of the spirits and man; the one half eternal, the other as ephemeral as all things man-made.

> 24. And now, be it done through sorcery or ties or any deed of cruelty done with iron, or be it done through gold or silver or lead, may it be unbound and not persist; be it in a white pelt or in a

stained one, may it be unbound from your servant... 25. And be it in fields of crops or in the burden of the animals who stand on their feet; or be it the birds or be it the fishes, unbound may it be from the soul and body of your servant... 26. And be it a spell, or be it done in a tree, or in a fruit tree, may everything be unbound from your servant... 27. And be it in a shell or in a stone, and be it in the grave of a Mussulman (Tanbalat) or in the grave of Jew, or be it in a grave of children, or be it in the grave of a foreigner, or be it in the grave of the dead, or be it in the grave of a Christian, or be it in the grave of Anchorites, or be it in the grave of the lowly, or be it in the grave of a leader over the people, or in a (water)hole that has gone dry, or in a spring gushing forth, or in a canal of the ocean, unbound may everything be from the soul and the body of your servant... 28. And be it in the height, or in the ground (floor), or be it on the field, or be it in a vineyard, or be it in an entrance, or be it in the depths, unbound may everything be from the soul and the body of your servant... 29. And if it has been crafted in one of the stars, or as an idol from wax, or in the leaven, or in the date palm (Hosa'na), or in the palm (Dagua'le), unbound may everything be from the soul and the body of your servant... 30. And be it in a wall, or in a hinge; or be it in the ashes of the kitchen, or be it in a stone in the dwelling, or be it in the oven, unbound may everything be from the soul and the body of your servant.

Verses 24 to 30 should be of particular interest to any practising magician. The seven verses have a lot to say on how talismanic (black) magic was performed in the days of our author. *Materia magica*, objects and substances ritually used to create a binding spell, could be taken from any or all of the four realms: human, plant, animal, and mineral. And they could be placed in a great many different kinds of secret places to remain hidden while staying close to their target. Spells could be formed as idols made from wax or dough, or as amulets written on bark or leaves, small enough even to push behind the hinges of a door.

Obviously we are reminded here of the original story of Cyprian the Mage. Each of the demons conjured by him needed our saint to put a certain magical substance on the actual doorframe of Justina's house for the demon to gain access to her chambers.

31. And everything evil done against a man whose name we have called out, and whose name we have not called out, may all of that be expelled in the name of the God of Abraham ('Abraham) and Isaac (Yeshak) and Jakob (Ya'kob) the adored and glorified king; in his name may all of it be expelled from the soul and body of your servant N.N.. And may it be unbound from him any spell and any evil deed; may God open for him the portals of his mercy, and may the love of the Holy Spirit be granted to your servant... 32. Through the light of Christ that emerged from the mountain Tabor (Tabor) and appeared to the Apostle, and Moses (Muse) and Elias ('Elyas) arrived and a cloud shaded them. And by him who arrived and made the one made brittle by gout rise, and by him who

opened the eyes of the blind, who had been born (blind) from the womb, by him who walked over the sea, by him who tamed the power of the wind, and by him who made Saint Peter (Petros) walk out onto the ocean, and by him who purified the lepers, and by him who purified the woman whose blood was pouring, when she touched the seam of his gown and who had been ill for 30 years; by the light of the sun and by the beauty of the moon and by the circle of the stars and by the four Evangelists Matthew (Matewos) and Mark (Markos), Luke (Lukas) and John (Johannes); and by the intercession of the pure mother of light, Maria (Maryam); and by the legates and saints and by all martyrs, especially (firstly) Stephanus ('Estifanos) and by Georg (Giyorgis) and by Kosmas

(Kozmos) and Damianus (Dimyanos) and Theodoros (Tewodros) and Korestyos, and by the martyrs who were sentenced in Mastamya and Matalala, and Mercurius (Markoryos) and Gregor (Gorgoryos) and Athanasius ('Atnatyos) and 'Akseyos and Philotheus (Felteyos) and Mercurius and Belyamen and Abraham; and by all scriptures of God and all saints whom we have called out and whom we have not called out, and by the women who are adorned with fragrances, Barbara (Barbara) and Helena ('Eleni), the queen, and the saint 'Arsima; and by all saints and by the blood of the faithful and by the fight of the martyrs. I conclude this scripture by the power of Jesus Christ, the son of the living God, and by his cross, the life-giver, and by the testament of Saint Peter, the first of the Apostles, and by John the Hermit, who was put into prison, by the plea of Antonius ('Entones), the first of the monks, and by Daniel (Dan'el), Isaac (Yeshak) and Jacob (Ya'kob), whom they cut off; and by the prayer of the prophets and by the prayer of all faithful martyrs whom I have unbound. Unbind, therefore, from the soul and body of your servant who carries this book, every knot and binding and sorcery, and every devilish thing expel from your servant in eternity. Amen.

In verse 32, as with verse 23, the magical act is firmly placed into the Biblical lineage, this time that of Jesus and the four Evangelists, as well as the Christian martyrs who followed them.

What requires highlighting is the short section before the last sentence. Here our ritualist calls upon the blessing and support of "all faithful martyrs whom I have unbound." This section could explain some of the ambiguous language in many earlier verses. Even in the original German version, it is almost impossible to tell whether the ritualist is calling on the named powers for help, or whether they are praying so that those powers themselves may be unbound. The relationship seems to be thought of, ideally, as a mutual one: anybody called on for help is also included in being released from any binding spell that may have been put on them at an earlier time. After all, isn't this how magical lineages work? Any act of one link affects the entire chain. And in the end, it's the entire chain that is "the giant on whose shoulders we stand."

Conclusion

What is humbly called *Oratio Cypriani*, "A Prayer of Cyprianus," on closer examination reveals itself to be a powerful, general ritual exorcism of the entire Judeo-Christian lineage (Schermann, p.19).

The date of the original source of the reconstructed Ethiopian version can be placed with relative certainty in the fourth century A.D.. Some scholars go so far as to assume that Cyprian of Antioch was the actual author of this prayer. Others, more conservatively, assume that this document was merely attributed to Cyprian, pseudoepigraphy being a common practise at the time with sacred manuscripts.

> As furthermore a similar Greek original forms the basis of the two Latin *Orationi*, we have sufficient reason to believe there to have been a common source for all of these pieces of formulas of folk sorcery

> which were assumed to have magical powers, and which are ascribed to the thaumaturge Cyprian of Antioch just as in the Old Testament the Psalms are ascribed to the singer-king David and the proverbs to the wise Solomon.
>
> — Karl Michel, p.22

A particularly outstanding feature of the *Oratio Cypriani* is the confluence of ancient pagan and early Christian spiritual beliefs that it contains. The strong spiritual desire for purification that marked the period from the second to the fourth century A.D. finds a unique expression in the *Oratio Cypriani*'s leveraging of ancient pagan exorcism techniques to bring about its desired result.

It is only through the customary use of exorcism as acknowledged by Tertulian, Origen, and Celsus amongst the people in ancient Christian times—which was closely connected to their understanding of angels and demons, and was intricately tied to their eschatology and their striving for moral purification and the forgiveness of sins—that we begin to understand these pseudo-Cyprianic prayers in the right light.

— Karl Michel, p.9

The *Oratio Cypriani* thus belongs to a specific category of liturgical text that transcends the classical form and heavily borrows from the genre of pagan conjurations such as those found in the Greek Magical Papyri.

As we can find the characteristics of exorcistic prayers in the pseudo-Cyprianic Orationi, we will not be wrong in perceiving them as conjuration prayers or magical hymns that aim towards liberation and purification.

— Karl Michel, p.15

Finally, the liturgical form of Cyprian of Antioch himself, as we encounter him in this magical prayer, has to be highlighted. Most likely the *Oratio Cypriani* is the earliest record in which Cyprian of Antioch is called upon as the keeper of a magical threshold: as an intermediary between the aspirant and the genuine sources of spiritual power stored in the Judeo-Christian lineage.

Let's recall what we discovered in the previous chapter about the original tomb of our magical saint, the *confessio* underneath the church SS Giovanni e Paolo. On the wall of his tomb we encountered the symbol of this threshold in the form of a praying saint looking directly at the ritualist. Now it is not unlikely that in the *Oratio Cypriani* we have discovered the actual magical hymn that was ritually performed in this sacred space.

Later so prominently adopted in the New World tradition of St. Cyprian, here we see the deepest ends of the roots of our magical saints.

We highlighted earlier that Cyprian of Antioch does not stand at the crossroads between the human and spiritual worlds, but rather that his body literally creates this threshold. In ritually assuming the body of St. Cyprian in the *Oratio Cypriani*, it was precisely this threshold that the ritualist activated and opened to his ritual actions.

Thus, in the *Oratio Cypriani* we have discovered one of the earliest forms of ritual magic performed by physically turning oneself into the spiritual threshold called "a saint." Praying to a saint, then, as is still common in private and public Catholic devotions today, is an act of calling up a threshold. Performing a ritual hymn such as the *Oratio Cypriani*, however, reveals the true underlying magical power of working with saints: it invites the practitioner to step away from his mortal self and, for the duration of the conjuration, to become the saint.

> Here we encounter the earliest impulses of the religious desire of the public which later lead to the intercessory prayer to the saints, while initially the appeal was done in the actual name of the righteous.
>
> — Karl Michel, pp.16–17

The Grimoire of Cyprian

a Coptic erotic love spell

In recent years much has been written about magic's magnificent rise from the ashes as a field of academic interest. After decades of scholarly disregard and disdain, we have seen a flood of academic publications on Medieval and Renaissance magic, in particular since the early 2000s.

Frank Klaassen's 2013 *The Transformations of Magic: Illicit Learned Magic in the Later Middle Ages and Renaissance* so far offers the most concise insights into this academic paradigm shift of not only looking at magical (written) artefacts for their historical interest, but also for their expression of a genuine Western spiritual tradition.

The late nineteenth and early twentieth centuries experienced a similar, if not more remarkable, blossoming of scholarly interest in magic. However, unlike today, the interest was directed at writings roughly a thousand years older than the medieval grimoires. Karl Preisendanz published the first two-volume edition of the Greek Magical Papyri in 1928 and 1931; Angelicus Kropp in the same year finished a similar Herculean task—which is much less well known in English speaking countries—by translating and editing three volumes of Ancient Coptic Magical Texts.

It was during the same period that, in 1934, Alfred Bilabel and Friedrich Grohmann published their two-volume work, *Greek, Coptic and Arabic Religious Texts from Egypt's Late Period*. Much criticized for its imperfect translation (see Polotsky), it nevertheless contained the first full version of what has come to be known as the *Grimoire of Cyprian* (*Cyprian's Zauberbuch*).

> The Grimoire of Cyprianus belongs to the series of grimoires purchased in the 1930s (by the university of Heidelberg). The find spot is unknown.

The paper, which contains various conjurations and sorcery-intercessions in the Coptic language directed towards the mighty magician Cyprianus, is made from rag paper. The booklet consists of four double pages (16 pages). A page numbering does not exist. Remains of the binding still exist in the form of a thread. Dating is within the 11th century.

— Moßner Nauerth, p.48

Sixty-five years later, in 1999, Howard M. Jackson contributed an English translation of this long and fascinating conjuration to the wonderful book *Ancient Christian Magic: Coptic Texts of Ritual Power (ACM)*.

In the introduction above, we eluded to the daemonic nature of Cyprian the Mage. We explained how his nature was equally material and spiritual. Cyprian once was a human being; yet in his current form his body is made of fire and resides in the spiritual realm. Cyprian thus is a bridge between two seemingly separate worlds. One of the *formae nativae*, he is a mediating principle that, once we connect with it, allows us to travel back and forth between the many realms to which his compound body forms a gateway.

As we will see when examining the *Grimoire of Cyprian*, this ambiguity—or polarity, to be more precise—not only affects the nature of Cyprian's spirit body, but also expands into the ethical realm. Like all sources of raw power, Cyprian is neither good nor bad: he knows no morals but the ones we offer up to him. All things will pass over his threshold as long as the ritualist knows how to access it. Just as nature doesn't judge whether we shape a shovel or a sword from its iron ore, so Cyprian doesn't judge how the powers he offers are used. Like all ancient spiritual beings, our saint simply *is*.

Hadean Press' author José Leitão eloquently described this moral polarity—or the complete absence thereof—in a recent Rune Soup podcast, in which he used the relationship of St. Bartholomew with the Devil to illustrate their interdependence. The same polarity can be discovered within the body of St. Cyprian, as we will see:

> This duality of St. Bartholomew and the Devil suggested there is a very concrete connection between both of them. And in my own perspective—taking some liberties with St. Bartholomew's iconography—St.Bartholomew and the Devil, they are each other's skin. When you remove one layer, then the other one is there; if you remove that one, than the other one is there.
>
> — José Leitão on *Rune Soup*,
>
> 11th August, 2016

Chapter 2. Cyprian of Two Worlds

Examining the *Grimoire of Cyprian*, we find it really contains a single erotic spell. Just as in the previous *Oratio Cypriani*, the ritualist takes the position of Cyprian himself and slips under the 'skin' of our magical saint.

> I know that everything has passed me by. Everything has changed in my soul; everything has changed in my person. My heart has grown bitter. I have grown pale. My flesh shudders; the hair of my head stands on end. I am all afire. I have lain down to rest, but could not sleep; I have arisen, but I found no relief. I have eaten and drunk in sighting and groaning. I have found no rest either in soul or in spirit for being overwhelmed by desire. My wisdom has deserted me; my strength has been sapped. All contrivance has been brought to naught. Yet I am Cyprian, the great magician, who was the friend

of the dragon of the abyss. He called me his son, and I called him father. He placed his crown and his diadem on my head. I suckled milk at his right breast. He made my place at this right hand. (...)

— *ACM*, p.154

The beginning of the spell emulates the tone of the *Confessio*, one of the first books to tell of Cyprian's story. We encounter a rueful magician, once adorned with great powers and sitting next to the "dragon of the abyss," who now has paid the price for his haughtiness and heresy. But instead of then telling a tale about his conversion, the spell mentions nothing of Cyprian's departure from his magical faith. Quite the opposite. The consequence of his failed attempts to conquer the heart of Justina by daemonic help is a renewed effort of his magical practice:

> So I reproved my wrath, laid my anger aside, and allayed my rage with great humility. Then I got to my feet, turned my face to the west, stretched my right hand out to heaven, cleansed myself of dirt on my feet, snorted, and directed these spells at heaven, to the tabernacle of the father within the seven veils. I cried out to the father of the aeons, the lord of every lordship, of every power and every throne, voicing the following spells: ERISI TONAI CHARIM BALIM, O king, AUTOUL OBIA KAKIKEPHALI AMOU AMOU!
>
> — *ACM*, pp.154–155

What follows is a coercive conjuration of the archangel Gabriel. Then this angel is made to take the role previously held by the pagan daemons, and magically pressured into taking possession of the heart, soul, and spirit of an anonymous young woman in order to bring her under Cyprian's spell and fill her with "burning desire."

Thus in the *Grimoire of Cyprian* we discover a curious turn of the narrative plot. In this case, Cyprian's failure to bring Justina under the spell of his pagan daemons results in a change of techniques rather than ethics. Pragmatically, Cyprian concludes that Christian magic outweighs his pagan practice, so rather than invoke another daemon, he instead performs the very same erotic love spell, but coerces Gabriel into doing the job instead.

In making this rather unexpected narrative turn, however, this *Grimoire* hardly stands alone. The first Christian centuries were more a battleground of worldviews and spiritual currents than ethics and morals. In many cases, the new Christian ideas landed on fertile pagan soil. And rather than replacing a pantheistic magical worldview, Christianity simply integrated itself into it. After all, the greatest of all magical powers is to create a synthesis of seeming opposites—or in other words, to make the serpent bite its tail.

In his 1935 article on Bilabel and Grohmann's edition of *Coptic Spells*, Hans Jakob Polotsky complains about the synergetic and subversive tendencies of magic:

> What is most repellent about these texts—despite their interest from a historic and religious perspective—is the self-indulgence with which the sorcerer is bringing the relevant biblical material into the required analogy for the verminous intent of his clients. The perverse rawness of the thought that one (...) could turn to Gabriel, or by the conjuration of the nails of the Cross one could bring on a scorpion to sting, must mark the extreme rock bottom not only of Coptic, but of all (...) magic.
>
> — Polotsky, 1935, p.425

Actually, we might want to take a closer look at the story of Christ conjuring a scorpion by the nails of his own Cross. Rather than being the nadir of magic, in my eyes it seems a wonderful artefact of ancient magical pulp fiction, with magicians creating a deliberately fake genre to ridicule the stupidity of their clients and test how far they could push their masquerades while still charging money for them. Polotsky is obviously judging this material from his own Christian bias, and entirely misses its obvious humour and sarcasm. Even the famous SATOR formula at the end seems deliberately misspelled.

> (...) He (Jesus) walked with Michael and Gabriel and Raphael and the Twelve Apostles and the twenty-four elders at the door of Paradise. He found a fainted worm lying on the ground. He spoke to it: "What is it with you?" It spoke to him: "O Lord, Jesus Christ, as soon as I saw you I was so afraid." He spoke to it:

> "Don't be. Don't be afraid, but rise and bite the one called Emla. — I conjure you today, male scorpion and female scorpion, in the name of the Father, the Son, and the Holy Ghost. I conjure you by the five nails, which were pierced into Christ and whose names are: Sator Areto Tenet Otera Rotas, (...)."
>
> — Polotsky, 1935, p.421

Conclusion

On looking into the mirror that is Cyprian the Mage, we see ourselves just as much as we see a goët or a theurgist. Whether our source of spiritual power stems from above or below, and whichever way we choose to direct its force, the image in the mirror does not judge. Our saint is a true hybrid: half human, half spirit; half pagan, half Christian. In uniting both fleshes, both bloods, both spirits within one gestalt, Cyprian neutralizes any morality and any ethical bias. He is the hand that hands us the key, the sword that points the way.

For a moment let's imagine having St. Cyprian as our magical teacher. We would need to learn quickly how to walk all by ourselves. To conduct ourselves without false empathy or any cushioning. He would neither harm us nor protect us. We might perceive him as a grim, cold man, almost inhuman, giving us everything we ask for, even if we are not remotely ready for it.

And here, Cyprian the Mage personifies one of the most important qualities that any neophyte must adopt on their magical path: that of taking full responsibility for themselves. Not only for their actions and words, but also for their desires and secret wishes. Cyprian the Mage will open for us any door upon which we choose to knock. And he will keep on giving until we are buried under the weight of our wishes or burned down by the flames of our heart.

As we will see in the next chapter, it is precisely this quality of his that has remained stable and continuous over the many centuries of our magical saint's history. The books and manuscripts assigned to his name might seem spurious and random at first glance. Yet if we look for this defining quality—the willingness to offer healing and harm in equal measure—then we will begin to see the defining part of St. Cyprian's tradition, and maybe even of our whole Western Magical path. It is the ultimate poison.

From the stories of Apuleius of Tyana and the Medieval Faust, to the Late Renaissance John Dee and the modern Aleister Crowley, a life lived in the pursuit of magic always requires one to learn how to handle this poisonous flask. Whatever standards we choose to adopt—left hand, right hand, or simply our own hand—magic is an assiduous poison that finds every fissure and crack in our desires and deeds. The judgement applied is not one of human morals, though, but one of organic repercussions. Once we conjure powers into our human vessel that were never meant to fill it, then the cup must carry the burden.

Hegel held that a thing can arise only through its opposite, and this is precisely how Cyprian the Mage helps us push forward on our magical path. Having sat next to the dragon in the abyss as well as having lost all his powers to be left behind in shuddering flesh, there is no longer any such thing as success or failure in the presence of our saint. Inside every vision is concealed a fear, and every fear conceals a vision. Walking alongside our saint, with each step he hands us a weapon yet takes away a piece of our armour. Until we stand naked and *see*, the next strike of our sword will bring destruction upon us as much as it will destroy anything else.

Chapter Three

Cyprian of Folk Magic

a mage of many faces

In the previous chapter we saw how Cyprian the Mage reacts to our intent and actions. We began to see him as a truly living saint, fluid and ambiguous in nature, always mirroring the image placed in front of him. He will readily reveal the devil under his skin if asked to; yet he will also protect and heal us, if that is our expressed intent. What he will never do, however, is to protect us from ourselves or the consequences of our wishes.

We realized this central nature of our magical saint by comparing Ethiopian and Coptic ritual spells from the fourteenth and eleventh centuries respectively, which used the power and advocacy of Cyprian of Antioch in opposite ways.

Now, the following document will help us develop a much deeper understanding of the uniquely ambivalent quality of Cyprian the Mage. It couldn't be more different from the spells examined previously, both in its literary form and in its time and place of origin. It also has never before been published in English.

Its author, Theodor Storm (14 September 1817—4 July 1888) was born in the small town of Husum on the southwest coast of the Duchy of Schleswig. Schleswig only became a part of Germany in 1884, and during most of Storm's lifetime it was under the administration of the Danish monarchy. Today, Storm is held to be one of the most important German representatives of poetic realism. In addition to his poems, his many novellas particularly contributed to his fame. Storm's most famous work, the novella *Der Schimmelreiter*, is often

Chapter 3. Cyprian of Folk Magic

Theodor Storm

used as a school text in Germany, and it has been made into a movie several times.

> Of the magical healing methods of the people, of sympathetic folk magic, Theodor Storm knew quite a few things and wove them into his novels.
>
> — Gratopp, p.64

From childhood on, living in the most northerly part of present day Germany, Storm was exposed to the folklore of the region, and continued to spend considerable time researching it as an adult.

> With his enthusiasm for all aspects of local folklore and superstition, his early boyhood was fired by the tales and legends recounted to him by Tante Brick and Lena Wies. Storm started collecting folk songs and folktales, rhymes and riddles and legends at an early age, and

maintained the interest for the rest of his life. He appears to have been an unusually consistent and systematic collector.

— Artiss, p.xiv

In 1862, next to many other works, Storm began work on three fairy tales which were published in 1865 and never received much public attention. In stark contrast to some of his works, which are still read at public schools today, these fairy tales remain so obscure and forgotten that their characters aren't even listed in Storm's full character index in the *Online Literary Lexicon*. Unsurprisingly, neither of the tales have ever been translated into English.

It's amongst these that we find a fairy tale with the title *The Mirror of Cyprianus*.

> The central motif of the tale is the evil woman who, guided by selfish motives, orders the killing of innocent children—depending on the original

source, either to secure the love of another man or to secure succession for her own son—and in the end is bitterly punished for her deeds. This plot was well known in Storm's time, as it was published as *Herzogin von Orlamünde* in the famous collection of short novels *(Des Knaben) Wunderhorn.*

— Gratopp, p.16

What is of particular interest about this tale for our study, however, is not so much its central motif, which Storm took from the most famous collection of folklore stories of the nineteenth century, published by Clemens Brentano and Achim von Arnim between 1805 and 1808, but the underlying narrative plot which forms the framework of the entire tale. Here we reencounter our magical saint, Cyprianus, now in the disguise of a wise sorcerer from the North, who crafts a huge magical mirror for a duchess after she saves his life. Over the course of the tale Cyprianus becomes one with the magical mirror, and it is through its image and impact that our saint becomes the moral heart of the story.

We will delve into the magical detail of the tale in good time. But first, let's lean back in our soft, cushioned theatre seats, see the lights dim, watch the curtain rise, and enjoy the show. Here is a most magical tale, the first ever English translation of *The Mirror of Cyprianus* by Theodor Storm:

The Mirror of Cyprianus

by Theodor Storm, 1862

The count's palace—actually it was a castle—rested high on the cliff. The crowns of ancient pines and oaks stretched up from deep below, and above them, and above the woods and the meadows, shone the splendour of spring. Inside, though, sadness ruled, as the count's only son was beset by illness, and even the noblest of doctors called upon could not tell the source of the evil.

The young boy lay pale-faced in the veiled chamber, deep in sleep. Two women sat either side of him with sorrowful faces, one of them old and in the dress of a servant, the other unmistakably the lady of the house, and almost young herself, though with the traces of past mourning in her pale, kind face.

In the most cherished days of his youth the count had courted her, a woman of little means. But when all that was missing was a spoken word, he had turned away from her. A rich, beautiful lady, jealous of the poor woman, had entrapped the noble count, a sanguine man, in her net of love; and while she had moved into the castle as the lady of the house, the other was left behind in her widow mother's parlour.

Yet the rich lady's good fortune had been fleeting. After a period of one year she had given birth to little Kuno, and while she was still on her birth-bed she was

Chapter 3. Cyprian of Folk Magic

reaped (killed) by a hot fever. After another year had passed, the count knew no better mother's hand for his young son than that of the woman he had once scorned. And she, with her calm heart, forgave him all hurt and became his wife.

And so she now sat, sorrowful, at the bedside of her child, a child which had been born to her rival.

"He is asleep now, and calm," the old nursemaid said. "The countess should rest as well."

"Oh no, nana," the gentle woman replied. "I have no need of rest yet. I am sitting comfortably in this cushioned chair."

"But all these long nights! It can never be called a sleep if one does not get out of one's clothes." And after a while she added: "There has not always been such a stepmother in this house."

"Please don't praise me so, nana."

"But don't you know the tale of the mirror of Cyprianus?" the old handmaid replied. And when the countess said no, she continued: "So let me tell you his story, for it will dispel your thoughts. And look how the child is sleeping now: his breath is going just fine and quiet from his mouth. Put this cushion behind you, now put your feet up on this stool... and now wait a little, while I remember it properly."

Then, when the countess had taken her seat in the cushions and kindly nodded to the handmaid, the old woman of the house began her tale.

"More than a hundred years ago, a countess once lived in this palace whom all the people called only 'the good countess.' And quiet right this name was, too: she was humble in her heart, and never looked down upon the poor and the low. Yet she was not a bright or happy countess. When she went to visit the houses of the youngest mothers down below in the village, she looked sorrowfully upon the handful of children who often blocked the doorways, and she thought: "What would I not give for just a single one of these chubby angels!" She had lived for more than ten years with her lord, and yet her marriage

Chapter 3. Cyprian of Folk Magic

remained without blessing; and neither to her had been given, as it has to your grace, a motherless child to whom she could have bestowed the treasure of her love. The count, a righteous and faithful man, had begun to look dark and worried, for no heir to his reign had yet come upon him. Good lord!" The storyteller interrupted herself. "And the rich hope for this, while the poor secretly hope to have one or two of their many angels up in the heavens, praying down for the others."

"Go on," her lady asked, and the old one continued:

"It was in the last days of the Great War, when this castle was often overcast by friendly as well as enemy forces, that it happened, one day, that an old doctor, who had come into this country with the Swedes, was wounded in a fight—there, at the back of the forest—by an Imperial bullet as he watched over his field hospital. The man, whose name was Cyprianus, was carried up to the castle and nursed with devotion by the good countess. She had a lucky hand, yet much time passed before the doctor was healed. Peace was declared, yet the countess still found herself walking beside the recovering old man in the small herb garden within the castle walls, listening to him speak of all the powers and secrets of nature. Many a sign and many a remedy from the mountains he passed on to her, and later these did much good to the ailments she attended. And thus it was that a thankful friendship was built between the beautiful woman and the wise old master.

It was at this time, too, that the Count, who had spent a year in the Emperor's army, returned to his castle. Once the joy of reunion had passed, the doctor, with his searching gaze, thought he recognized the mark of a quiet sorrow on the face of the kind countess. Yet the modesty of age still held back the question from his lips. And then, one day, he witnessed a crone of the black travelling people, who roamed the entire realm of Duke Michael, slipping

Chapter 3. Cyprian of Folk Magic

out of the countess' chamber. That evening, on their promenade through the tiny herb garden, he took her hand and addressed her keenly:

"You know, madame, I have a fatherly heart for you. So tell me, what was it that, today, around noon, while the count was asleep, you asked of that dire pagan in your chamber?"

The good countess was startled; yet when she saw the mild face of the old man she said: "I am in deep distress, Master Cyprianus, and I wish to know if a time shall come when these sorrows will be taken off me."

"So open up your heart to me!" he replied. "It may just be that I have better counsel than those travelling people, who know far more about the deceit of the credulous than the days of the future."

After the old man had spoken, the countess confided her sorrow to the old master, and how she was afraid that her childlessness might even lose her the heart of her husband.

They were passing by the wall enclosing the garden, and Cyprianus's gaze wandered out over the woods below that were ablaze in the late afternoon light.

"The sun is setting," he said, "and when she rises again on the morrow I shall be on my journey to my native land. But I owe you life and health, so let me ask you to accept the gift that I will send you, passed on by safe hands."

"You really have to go, Master Cyprianus?" the woman said in grief. "My most beloved comforter will part from me!"

"Don't be sad, Countess," he replied. "The gift I speak of is a *speculum*, a mirror in other words, crafted under a special crossing of the stars and at the most fortuitous time of year. Placed in your chamber and used as ladies are wont to use mirrors, it will bring you better lore than the treacherous pagans of the heath. They think of me," the old man added, smiling mysteriously, "in my native land, as hardly

Chapter 3. Cyprian of Folk Magic

ignorant of anything that is of nature."

But there the old storyteller stopped herself. "You must know, dear Countess, that in later days Cyprianus was renowned as a powerful sorcerer in all the northern countries. After his death, the books written in his hand were chained up and buried deep in the crypt of a castle, for people believed they contained evil things which threatened the salvation of the soul. But those who did so were mistaken, and not pure-hearted themselves; for, as Cyprianus pointed out often while staying in this house, the forces of nature are never evil in a righteous hand.

"But let me continue with my story. Several moons passed after the master had left the castle, having given consoling words to husband and wife. Then, one day, an old cart with a large wooden chest stopped in the courtyard. The count and countess, who had seen its arrival from the window high above, driven by their curiosity, quickly descended and were handed by the old wagoner a letter written by Cyprianus on fine parchment. The chest, indeed, held the promised gift.

"May—" that's what the letter said "—this mirror add as many days of joy to your life as it has cost me hours of holy work. Yet forget not that the end of every affair is always in the hand of the fathomless God. And fend against but one thing: never let the image of a bad deed fall into this mirror. The beneficial forces which aided its creation would then become their mirror image. Especially for children—which may surround you soon, blessed be God—this would pose a deadly danger; and then, only atonement through the gushing of the culprit's own blood could restore the mirror's virtue. But your house has such grace that this could never happen; mayhap you will accept this gift from the hand of a grateful friend."

And just as the master had intended it, in hope and trust the husband and wife received his gift. Once the chest had been carried into the hall and opened, they saw at first a large frame, crafted all from bronze; then, when the mirror was lifted up, a tall, slender glass that shimmered a miraculous blue.

"Doesn't it seem, dear husband," said the countess as she took her first glance into the mirror, "as if the entire world rested within this mirror, under a gentle moonshine?"

Its frame was of sanded steel and the light, trapped and broken in its thousand facets, sparkled like colourful fire.

Soon the creation was set up in the bedchamber of the countess and her husband; and every morning, while the handmaid braided her blonde hair or rolled it into a bun, the good lady sat with folded hands in front of the mirror of Cyprianus and gazed, devoutly and full of hope, at her own reflection. And when the early morning sun began to shimmer on the facets of the frame, the reflection of the woman seemed to sit surrounded by a crown of stars. Often, after his first walk through the meadow and the woods, her husband would return to their chamber and sit silently behind her chair; and every time she saw him reflected in the mirror she thought his gaze had become gloomy again.

One morning some time later, the countess, the handmaid having left, thought she might like to take another look into the mirror. Yet a mist appeared on its glass so that she couldn't see her face. She took a cloth and tried to rub it off, but it was no good; and then she realized that the cloud was not on the glass at all, but deep inside it. When the countess peered closely into the mirror her face appeared clearly again; yet when she stepped away from it, it seemed as though a rosy glimmer hung between her and her reflection. Deep in thought, she put away the cloth and wandered aimlessly, but filled with a quiet prescience, through the large house.

Her husband, encountering her in the hallway, asked: "And why such a blessed smile, my dear?" And keeping silent, she wrapped her arms around his neck, and kissed him.

Every day now, after her husband and her handmaid had left the chamber, she stood alone before the Mirror of the Master; and every passing morning the rosy cloud shone more clearly behind the glass.

And so May arrived, and then one morning, as the scent of flowers in bloom streamed through the open window, the countess stepped in front of the mirror again. Hardly had she looked than she heard herself crying "Alas!" and her hands rushed to her heart; for as the morning's spring sun illuminated the mirror she recognized at once the face of the sleeping child that hung in the rosy cloud. She stood holding her breath; yet she could not turn away from the image she beheld in the mirror.

That's when she heard the blowing of horns from out over the fields: it was her husband returning from the hunt. She closed her eyes and stood patiently until, followed by their dog, he entered the chamber.

Then she laid her arms around him and, pointing to the mirror, she said in a whisper: "the heir of your house is greeting you." Now the husband also recognized the small face in the rosy cloud, and the shimmer of joy quickly waned from his face. The countess saw in the mirror how the count paled. "Don't you see it?" she whispered.

"I see it, my dear," the count replied. "But it frightens me to see the child crying."

She turned to him and shook her head. "You foolish man," she said. "It is sleeping, even smiling in its dream."

And that is how it was for both of them. He walked in sorrow as she, with the help of the midwife, prepared the cradle next to the down-filled cushions and the delicate, small clothes of the house's future heir. Sometimes, when she stood in front of the mirror, she reached out for the rosy cloud in dreamlike longing; but when her fingers touched the cold surface of the glass, she lowered her arms and

CHAPTER 3. CYPRIAN OF FOLK MAGIC

thought of the words of Cyprianus: "All things must be given their due time."

And yet her hour also arrived. The cloud in the mirror waned—and instead, a rosy boy rested on the white linen of her bed. This brought much happiness into the castle and into the village down below, and when the count rode through his bright meadows in the morning he pulled on the reins of his Goldfox and shouted merrily into the sunshine, "I have a son!"

As was the custom, six weeks after giving birth the countess visited church, and from that day on people saw her regularly again, coming down into the village to the houses of the poor. Only now her gaze did not rest sorrowfully on the children of the peasants; instead, she often stood for a long time inclining towards them, and advised them in their games; and where she saw a very strong boy, she thought to herself, "mine is still stronger than him."

However, as Cyprianus had written, the end of every affair is still in the hand of the mysterious

God. Come autumn, an evil fever descended upon the village. People died, and before that they lay on their beds calling desperately for help. The good countess did not wait to answer their calls. With the arcane secrets of the old master she went into each cottage. She sat at the bedside of the dying, and with her cloth, when their time of departure arrived, she took off the final sweat from their brows.

And then, when little Kuno was scarcely half a year old, Death, from whom she had stolen away many lives, walked back with her up into the castle. And after her cheeks had burned like dark roses in her fever, at last Death made her cold and pale on her bed.

Then all joy was exhausted. The count rode with lowered head over his meadows and let his steed go whichever way it chose. "Now I know why my poor boy had to cry even before his own birth," he told himself. "One is in a womb but once in the whole world."

CHAPTER 3. CYPRIAN OF FOLK MAGIC

Lonely stood the mirror in the bed-chamber; and however often the morning sun sprinkled its sparks on its glittering frame, the image of the countess never appeared in it again.

"Take it away," the count said one morning to the old caretaker, "its brightness hurts my eyes!" The caretaker had the mirror carried to a remote chamber on the highest floor, which at the time was used to store all sorts of weapons; and once the men who had carried it had gone, the old man took a black drape from the countess' funeral and covered the art of Master Cyprianus with it so that no ray of light could ever touch it again.

Yet the count was still young; and when a few years had passed and his strong son began to rampage through the long halls of the castle, the count thought to himself: "You should search for a mother for your son, one who will raise him according to the noble customs befitting your heir." And then he thought: "Many comely women are at the Emperor's court; it would be bad if you didn't pick the right one." And there was a voice in his ears that spoke: "A mother for your child, a woman for you; because a woman's love is a sweet potion!"

And so, once May had returned again, the court prepared for his journey; and together with his son, and accompanied by lordly service, they set off towards the large city of Vienna.

They were gone a long time. The old caretaker wandered through the high, empty chambers and had the windows opened so that the belongings of the countess would not perish in the stale air.

But at long last, as the autumn spiderwebs blew over the fields, many chests arrived in the castle that were filled with precious carpets, gold-pressed leather wallpapers, and all sorts of fashionable things the likes of which had never before been seen by the local servants; and the caretaker received his orders to prepare the large chambers for the new lady of the house."

Chapter 3. Cyprian of Folk Magic

Here the elderly narrator stopped for several moments, as the young sick boy had pushed away his duvet. After she had carefully tucked him in again, and the boy was sleeping peacefully once more, she continued her story:

"You have seen her, my lady: the life-size portrait of a woman hanging in the Knights' Hall, next to the fireplace, is supposed to be her likeness. A vixen with reddish gold hair, the sort of woman who always turns out to be dangerous, especially to older men. I have often looked at her. How she pulls back her head, how her lips smile so sweetly and connivingly—and how her hair streams in untamed love-curls down her white neck! A colder blood than that of the good count would have not been able to resist her. Let me just add this: she was a young widow and had a child from her first marriage, a young daughter, and there were relatives of her former husband in the Emperor's city. This much is certain: that daughter never came to see this castle.

Well, on we go! Finally the carriages rattled into the courtyard, and the assembled servants marvelled when the count and a lady-in-waiting of foreign tongue helped the countess down from the carriage. As she climbed the stairs, wearing a silk dress the colour of almonds, her ears pricked up as she heard some murmured words on the beauty of the new lady.

Only after she had disappeared through the castle gate did young Kuno climb from the servant's carriage, which had been following along behind. "Hey, boy," a red-cheeked maidservant called towards him, "you have a beautiful mother, now!" Yet the boy frowned and sullenly replied: "that is not my mother!" The old caretaker, who had just returned from accompanying his lordship, said to her sourly: "Can't you see this is the son of the good countess?" And looking deep into the boy's blue eyes, he picked him up and carried him into his father's house.

From then on, the foreign lady dwelt there. The servants praised her affability, and soon the peasants

CHAPTER 3. CYPRIAN OF FOLK MAGIC

in the village were saying that she was even more generous than the dead countess. Only she did not look after the children; neither could they bring their sorrows and needs to her as they had done to the previous countess.

While she allured most visitors to the castle with her beauty, the old caretaker had only cold looks for her. He disapproved of how, even on workdays, she walked, in his words, "adorned like a Jezebel." He did not trust how she would suddenly lavish her young stepson with caresses when she was in his and the count's presence.

And neither did she ever win over the boy's heart: he had nothing but a silent gaze for her, and when her arms and eyes set him free again, he would turn and run outside. Then he would fetch his small crossbow and shoot at a wooden bird the old caretaker had whittled for him, or sit in the parlour of his old friend and browse through a large book on the delights of hunting.

The good count, though, saw nothing but the beauty of his wife. When he entered a room and walked up to her, she stood smiling until he embraced her; and if she turned her beautiful neck towards the door then she would lift the little hand-mirror from the folds of her silk dress—it was attached to a golden chain on her girdle—and, gazing into it, merely nod towards the person entering.

When spring returned, a fever fell upon the boy. He had brought it home from the moist mosses of the woods, and now he lay in the fretful slumber of the afflicted. Next to his bed stood the old countess' chair, with its carved backrest and blue silk cushion, on which she had so often sat looking into Master Cyprianus' mirror as the breeze carried the scent of violets through the open window. Now, though the violets in the courtyard were blooming again, the chair was empty. The beautiful stepmother was there, though, sitting by the count at the foot of the little bed, for she saw how the father cared for his son and

Chapter 3. Cyprian of Folk Magic

it wouldn't have behoved her to be absent.

Suddenly the boy shouted from his fever: "Mother, mother!" and sat bolt upright, his eyes open.

"Listen, my husband!" said the beautiful woman, "our son is asking for me!" But when she stood to lean over him, the child stretched out his arms past her towards the empty chair of the good countess.

The count paled and, conquered by the pain of the sudden memory, sank to his knees by his son's bedside. The proud woman, though, stepped back and, her small fist tightly gripping her girdle, left the chamber never to return. Yet the boy recovered even without her care.

Soon thereafter, as the rosebuds were growing, the countess gave birth to a son. The count could not tell why his heart was so heavy when little Kuno ran up to him with the news. He had his steed saddled and led from the stables to ride out into the heath, not to call out joyously over the leas and lakes, but rather to catch hold of his thoughts.

He had just mounted when the old caretaker lifted up little Kuno to him and said: "Do not forget the son of the good countess!" The father embraced his son and rode with him over the country until sunset. Returning, as they passed the committal crypt, he made his steed slow down and murmured into his son's ear: "Do not forget her. One has a mother's love but once in the whole world."

When he entered the room where his wife rested, and a maid placed his newborn son into his arms, a longing for his dead first wife suddenly overcame him. At that moment he knew that she had been the only one ever to possess his heart. The boy in his arms, despite being his own blood, seemed alien, as he wasn't hers. The eyes of the countess, though she had risen with even more beauty than ever from her birthing bed, could bewitch him no longer.

Lonely he rode through the meadows, and the words of Master Cyprianus loomed as if in black letters before his eyes: "Living your life backwards

Chapter 3. Cyprian of Folk Magic

is impossible, even with God's help."

Meanwhile the two boys grew up together, and soon a deep love grew between them. Once little Wolf could come outside, Kuno became his teacher in all those arts practised by little boys. He had him climb over rocks and trees, nicked arrows for his little crossbow, and helped him shoot them at the mark, or even at some wild bird circling high above them, out of reach, in the splendour of the sun.

Once again winter had returned when, one night, a man dressed in the uniform of a field colonel rode with his servant into the courtyard. Gaunt was his name, and that's how he looked: a lean, bony man with an angular countenance and small, grim eyes. His shaggy straw yellow beard, so they say, stood like rays from his chin and nostrils. He called himself a cousin of the countess' first husband, and he had come, so he claimed, simply to visit. Yet he stayed at the castle for week after week, and slowly became one of its residents.

At first the count cared little for the visitor, but the colonel proved to be a master hunter, and once the first snow had fallen, both men went out into the fir tree forest. From this day on, almost daily, there was the uproar of dogs and the "Ho Ridoh!" of the hunters in the quiet woods.

Then, one afternoon, during a boar hunt, the colonel's horn was heard coming from a remote valley where he and the count had pushed ahead without their servants. When the dogs and the hunters following the call arrived, they saw the boar dying in between the firs, and, by it, the count lying in his own blood. The colonel stood leaning on his lance, the horn still in hand.

"Your hunting spears are no good," he said. "The boar has finished our sport."

Seeing them standing astonished in shock, he scowled at them with his grim, small eyes. "What are you looking at? Cut branches into a stretcher and carry your lord back to his castle!" And the people did as they were told.

The count never again rode out to hunt with the colonel. The old caretaker, sending a servant for a doctor to attend the wound, was told that this would not be necessary, for the count was already dead.

Soon he rested in the crypt by his good countess, and little Kuno was without father or mother. But the colonel remained in the castle, and the countess let piece after piece of the house's running pass into his hand. The servants grumbled when he barked at them with his sharp voice, but they didn't dare resist the grim man.

He also involved himself with the two boys. One morning, as Kuno came down to the stables, next to the colonel's tall horse stood a small, black horse. It was the sort of horse that came from the north, and it had a golden saddle. "This is yours," said the colonel, who had entered at the same time as Kuno. "Climb up and I'll show you how a man should ride."

Before long he also had acquired a horse for Wolf, and he took care to teach them both the whole art of riding. The gaunt colonel on his long-legged horse riding over the fields with his two young charges on their small northern steeds was soon a common sight.

But what he said to them on those rides was far from common. Once, when they, as happens with children, fell into quarrel, he leaned down from his high horse and whispered to the elder Kuno: "You are the lord, you can ban the fellow from the castle!" And then to Wolf on his other side: "He wants to show thee that thou ridest on his land!" These comments immediately stopped the boys' quarrel: they even climbed off their horses and fell into each others' arms crying!

The colonel was sharp-eyed, and clearly saw how the eyes of the beautiful countess darkened every time she saw her stepson walk with her own son through the door; and how her hostile looks remained for a little time even after their departure.

Chapter 3. Cyprian of Folk Magic

One sunny afternoon, the colonel and countess stood in her small garden, where the good countess had once listened to the wise words of Master Cyprianus. When the beautiful woman gazed out over the woods and down into the wetlands, he remarked testily: "Kuno will have a nice inheritance when his time comes." And when she remained silent, staring out through her dark eyes, he added: "Your Wolf is a delicate planting, while Kuno seems born for the regiment; he looks tough and hardened already."

Just at this moment, in the meadows below the garden, the two boys were flying along on their horses. They had been riding so closely together that the brown curls of Kuno had got tangled with little Wolf's blond ones. The latter's horse shook its mane and neighed in the sun. Seeing this, Wolf's mother startled and cried out, yet Kuno wrapped his arm around his brother; and as they rode by he glanced up with his bright eyes to the shadows of the countess and the colonel on the castle.

"How do you like his eyes, dear countess?" asked the colonel.

She paused and stared at him questioningly.

"What do you mean?" she murmured.

His hand on his chin, he replied: "Count on me, beautiful woman. Colonel Hager is your loyal servant."

When she whispered her answer, he saw how her face turned deathly pale. "I should like these eyes even better if they were closed."

"And what would you be willing to give for seeing them made so much more beautiful?"

For a moment she rested her white hand on his. Then she threw back her shiny curls and, not looking back, walked from the garden.

An hour later, young Kuno was roaming through the hallways of the higher floors, when he suddenly saw the colonel standing before him. The boy tried to pass by quickly, as the man looked so uncanny. Yet he was called upon: "Where are you running, boy?"

Chapter 3. Cyprian of Folk Magic

"To the old armoury," Kuno said. "I want to fetch my crossbow."

"Very well. I'll walk with you."

The colonel walked with the boy to the out-of-the-way room where, amongst all sorts of weaponry, and covered by a heavy cloth, the mirror of Cyprianus still stood. Once they had entered, the colonel moved the iron lock into place and leaned against the heavy door. When the boy saw the man's wild eyes, he cried: "Hager, Hager, you plan to kill me!"

"That is not a bad guess," the colonel replied, and lunged for him. The boy jumped away from his grasp and tore his crossbow from the wall where he had hung it only the day before. He shot—and you can still see the mark of his bolt in the black oak wall—but the colonel he missed.

The boy fell to his knees and cried: "Let me live! I shall give you my northern horse and even the beautiful saddle!"

The grim man stood before him, his arms crossed over his chest. "Your northern horse," he replied, "is not swift enough for me."

"Dear Hager, let me live!" the boy cried again. "Once I am all grown up, I'll give you my castle, and all of the beautiful woods I'll make yours as well!"

"All these I'll have even sooner," said the colonel.

The boy dropped his head. "Very well," he said. "Then I offer myself up to the eternal grace of God."

"That's the spirit!" said the evil man. But the boy jumped up once more and flew over the walls of the chamber. The colonel flew after him, hunting him like an animal.

But when they passed by the covered mirror, the boy's foot got entangled in the cloth and he fell hard to the ground. And there was the evil man above him!

Chapter 3. Cyprian of Folk Magic

At that very moment, so the story goes, as the colonel pulled back his fist for the killing blow and the little boy covered his heart with both hands, the old caretaker was standing in the far corner of the castle's cellar with a servant who was busy pulling a bottle of Ingelheimer from a barrel.

"Did you not hear that, Casper?" he said, setting down his lamp on the cask.

The servant said he had not.

"I felt," the old man said, "as if the boy Kuno had called my name."

"You must have been mistaken, master," the servant replied. "You can't hear a thing down here."

For a while they stood quietly in the cold, then the old man said again: "For God's sake, Casper, he has called me again! It was a cry for help from the boy's throat!"

The servant continued his work on the bottle. "All I hear is the wine pouring from the barrel," he muttered.

But the old man was not to be deterred. He climbed up into the castle and went from door to door, first on the ground floor and then through the upper levels.

When he reached and opened the door of the armoury, illuminated by the evening sun, the mirror of Cyprianus shone upon him. "Whose unholy hand has torn this down?" grumbled the old man. And when he lifted the cloth from the ground, he found the corpse of the boy, his dark curls over his closed eyes.

The old man fell to his knees. Crying, he lifted the dear boy into his arms. He pulled back the boy's clothes and looked for the mark of death. Yet he found nothing but a dark stain over his heart.

For a long time, grim and dark, he remained on his knees. Then he wrapped the boy in the black cloth, pulled him up into his arms, and carried him downstairs, towards the chamber of the countess.

Chapter 3. Cyprian of Folk Magic

Entering, he saw the proud woman standing close the colonel, deathly pale and shaking, the colonel forcefully holding onto her hand.

The old man laid the corpse between them and fixed his gaze on them. "The heir, count Kuno, is dead; your son, countess, is now heir to this county."

About a month after the funeral of the young heir, the countess was leaning on the parapet of the small balcony that led from her chamber, that let her step out and breath fresh air. Little Wolf stood by her, looking at a swarm of birds sitting and chirping in the tops of the pines and oaks below them.

"Look!" the countess said, pointing with her finger. "They are fighting off an owl: there he is, right by that knothole in that oak."

The boy's curious eyes followed her hand. "I see it well, mother," he said. "It is a deathly thing; it called out in front of my window when Kuno died."

"Grab your crossbow and shoot it!" his mother said.

The boy jumped back into the chamber, down the stairs, and into the stables. There the crossbow was, resting by his small horse. But the bowstring was torn; he hadn't used it for too long, as Kuno was no longer there to carve his bolts or attach the wooden bird to the high pole. So he ran back into the castle.

Wolf remembered how his brother had kept his own crossbow upstairs in the armoury, so he went to that dusty part of the castle and pushed himself through the tall oaken door.

The twilight room was lit by the blue shimmer of the mirror of Cyprianus. The iron features of its frame flashed in the last rays of the evening sun. The boy had never seen a sight like it before. Even when he had followed his brother up to the armoury, the mirror had always been covered by a heavy black cloth. Now he stood before it and marvelled at his reflection in the splendour. He seemed to have forgotten the crossbow entirely. Yet there was something else beside him in the mirror, something

Chapter 3. Cyprian of Folk Magic

that absorbed all his senses. He knelt down and, in order to get as close as possible, rested his forehead against the glass.

Suddenly he leaped back and pressed both his hands to his heart. With a cry he jumped up. "Help!" he yelled. "Help!" And a third time, in piercing pain: "Help!"

His mother, out on the balcony, heard his call. In mortal fear, she wondered from room to room, from door to door. Finally she arrived at the right door. There her boy lay on the floor, writhing in agony.

She knelt herself down over him: "Wolf! Wolf! What has happened?"

The boy's pale lips moved. "It hit me on the heart," he murmured.

"Who, who did this?" whispered the mother. "Wolf, just say one more word: who did this?"

The boy raised his finger and pointed to the mirror. Holding her dying son in her arms, she leaned forward and stared into the glass of Cyprianus. Terror crept over her face, and her pale eyes became as hard as diamonds. In the evening glow, cloaked in a cloud of mist, she saw the figure of a child. As if in sorrow it cowered on the ground, seemingly asleep. She turned around, looking fearfully at the chamber, but there was nothing but twilight in its far corners. Again, as if under a spell, with tense eyes, she looked back into the mirror.

The figure was still there.

Then she felt the head of little Wolf falling from her arms; and in the very same moment she saw a light smoke seep onto the glass of the mirror. Like a breath it ran over its surface. Then the glass became clear again, while behind it the little cloud pushed deeper into the reflection. Now, suddenly, in the depth of the mirror, she saw two little figures, made of mist, holding onto each other.

With a cry the countess jumped up. Her son rested motionless, his features waxen, on the floor, his open blue lips sealing his death. Tearing his silken

Chapter 3. Cyprian of Folk Magic

clothes open, she saw a dark stain over his heart just as she had seen over the heart of little Kuno.

"Hager, Hager!" she cried—for the secret of the mirror she did not know. "This is your fist! He too was in your way; but you are not the ruler in this house yet, and I swear you never will be!"

She walked downstairs and searched for him, but the colonel had gone out to hunt at a neighbouring castle and was not due back until tomorrow.

The death of even the last son of the count spread numb terror amongst the servants. They stood on stairwells and in halls and murmured; and when the countess appeared, they scuttled away, frightened.

Night rose. The corpse of little Wolf had been carried downstairs and lay stretched out on the bed in his chamber.

The countess found no rest by the dead. Under bright moonlight, when everyone was deep asleep, she climbed again up to the armoury. There she stood in front of the mirror, reflected in its mesmerizing blue shimmer, staring into its glass with stony eyes and wringing her hands. Then, as if on the run from a sudden terror, she ran from the chamber and through the halls until she reached the door of her bedroom. She threw herself against the door and slammed it shut.

So the night passed.

The next morning, the old caretaker was approaching the chamber of the countess when he heard fierce and harsh words coming from within. He recognized the voice of the colonel who had just returned; and soon the countess replied in a similar tone. These were words of lethal hate.

Shaking his head, the caretaker stepped back from the door. "These are the judgements of God," he said, and climbed further towards the top of the round tower, as he suddenly felt a need for fresh air.

He leaned over the parapet and looked down into the sunny morning. "How beautiful the woods are growing," he said to himself. "And all of them are dead! The good countess, the good count, my boy Kuno, and now even little Wolf."

Then he heard a horse being pulled from the stables. Shortly after, a gallop thundered over the drawbridge. Before long the gallop was on the path towards the woods, then under the crowns of the trees, and finally a flock of ravens flew into the air.

At that very moment the cries of women echoed up from below. The old man heard the cries from everywhere: the countess was lying in her own blood, beaten to death.

"Where is the colonel?" the caretaker demanded.

"Gone!" the stable master called, as he came up from the courtyard. "Together with his long-legged black horse!"

Quickly the old man organized the hunt; but before long all of them were back, their horses covered in foam, having achieved nothing.

"Well. Let us bury the dead," the caretaker said, "and send a messenger to the new owner of these wonderful lands."

"And that is what happened," concluded the storyteller. "Rule passed to an ancestor of your husband's, who was the closest in the blood. The old caretaker is said to have lived for many long years after that, down there in that little hut by the gate, a loyal servant at the crypt of his lords."

"That is a terrible tale!" the countess said as the nurse fell silent. "But did you not hear the name of the first husband of this tragic countess?"

"Of course," the old woman replied. "Her maiden name is engraved on the frame of that portrait." And then she said the name of one of the earliest noble families.

"How strange!" the countess said. "So she is *my* ancestor."

The old woman shook her head. "Impossible," she said. "You, my lady? From the blood of this evil woman?"

"It is most certain, nurse; when that daughter was left behind in Vienna, she became wife to one of my ancestors."

Chapter 3. Cyprian of Folk Magic

At that point, the conversation was interrupted by the entry of the doctor. The boy continued to lie in death-like slumber, and did not move even when the doctor took his hand, searching for a sign of life.

"He will get well again?" the countess asked, looking worriedly at the doctor's tight-lipped face.

"That is more than any mortal can tell," he replied. "But the countess must sleep; that certainly is necessary." When she resisted, he added: "Nothing will change before tomorrow for your boy. Rest assured, the nurse can take the watch."

At length the countess was convinced and went to her chamber. The doctor had to insist that he would not leave the house until she had gone to bed.

But when the old woman was alone with him, she asked: "Are you truly certain that the countess can sleep without worry?"

"For now she can, yes."

"And then, doctor?"

"Then, when your lady has rested, you must

prepare her well, for the boy will die."

The old woman gazed at the doctor steadily. "Is this most certain?" she asked.

"It is indeed. It would take a miracle to change his condition."

After the doctor had gone, instead of the countess a young servant shared the watch with the nurse. She leaned on the bed, looking into the pale face of little Kuno that was marked by death's sharp fingers. "A miracle!" she murmured a few times. "A miracle!"

For the boy had moved on his cushion. "Let me play with the children!" he whispered.

The old one stared at him. "With which children?" she asked quietly.

The boy repeated in the same, calm voice: "With the mirror children, nurse."

She almost cried out. "Unhappy child! You have looked into the mirror of Cyprianus. But he is in the sacristy, and the sacristy is covered with stone." She thought for a moment, then said to the girl, "Get me

Chapter 3. Cyprian of Folk Magic

Vincenz, Ursel!"

Vincenz, the groom, came. "Have you recently been in the chapel building?" asked the old woman.

"I am there every day."

"Are any of the walls of the sacristy damaged?"

"Yes, there was some damage fourteen days ago."

"Have you seen a mirror there?"

He remembered. "Oh, of course, there is one in the corner. The frame seems to be of steel, but the rust has eaten it."

The old woman gave him a large carpet. "Cover the mirror carefully," she said. "Then let it be brought into this chamber, but quietly, so that the boy does not wake."

Vincenz went. Presently he and a servant brought, all covered by a carpet, a tall object into the room.

"Is this the mirror, Vincenz?" the nurse asked; and when he agreed, she continued: "Place it right at the foot of the bed, so that little Kuno can look into it as soon as the carpet is removed."

After the mirror was in place and the servants had left, the old woman took her seat at the bedside again. "A miracle is needed," she said to herself.

Then she sat, with closed eyes, like a statue of stone. Invisibly inside her, though, hope and fear were fighting. She waited for the return of the countess; but how long must she wait until sleep would withdraw entirely and the woman would wake again?

That's when the door opened and the countess walked in. "I was not granted the lightest sleep, nurse," she said. "Pardon me! You are so loyal and good, more understanding even than I; and still I feel as though I am not meant to leave the side of my boy's bed."

For a long time the old woman didn't reply. "Tell me again, my lady," she said, her heart beating so heavily she could hardly speak, "are you indeed sure that the evil countess was your ancestor?"

Chapter 3. Cyprian of Folk Magic

"I am most certain. But why do you ask, nurse?"

The old woman stood up, and with a great tug tore the carpet from the mirror.

The countess cried aloud. "My child, my child, that is the mirror of Cyprianus!" But when she had cast a glance into the soft glow of the glass, she saw little Kuno lying inside it, on his pillow with his eyes open. She saw him smiling and the sign of life returned to his cheeks.

She turned round.

He was already upright, fresh and flowering.

"The children, the children!" he called out in a bright, ringing voice, and stretched out his arms towards the mirror.

"Where are they?" the countess asked.

"There, there!" the old woman said. "Look, they are smiling and nodding. Alas, they have wings; two angels it is!"

"What are you saying?" the countess said. "I cannot see them."

"There, there!" little Kuno called. "Oh," he added sadly, "but now they have flown away."

The old nurse sank to the chair. "Our Kuno is saved!" she cried, breaking out in loud sobs. "Your love has done this: it has lifted the curse from the work of the Old Master!"

But the countess stood and stared blissfully into the mirror. For a subtle cloud, rose in colour, hovered over its surface, from which, quite distinctly, the face of a slumbering child glimmered.

"Wolf it shall be called, if it is to be a boy," she whispered softly. "Wolf and Kuno! And let us pray, nurse, that they may be happier than those who bore their names before!"

The End

Chapter 3. Cyprian of Folk Magic

Three Wicked Tongues

Cyprian of the Flesh

The name Cyprian is well known in Schleswig-Holstein.

— Gratopp, p.68

As has been extensively documented in several of the recent publications on Cyprian of Antioch, our saint takes on an important role in the Nordic tradition of magical Black Books. In these, Cyprian of Antioch becomes his younger self, Cyprian of the North. This tradition was still very much alive in Denmark even in Storm's day. In one of his letters, we learn what he first heard about our magical saint:

> According to the legend, Cyprian was living on a Danish island and was even worse than the devil, who thus despised him after his death. That's when Cyprian

wrote nine grimoires, of which only one complete copy survived; but it was forged into chains by a count in Plöner Castle and was buried beneath it. Whoever reads the nine books will be addicted to the devil. That's what Storm learned in Husum about Cyprian.

— Gratopp, p.69

One of the more comprehensive descriptions of the Nordic folklore about the sorcerer Cyprian can be found in the second volume of J.M. Thiele's *Danish Folk Legends (Danmarks Folkesagn)*. As this was published in 1843, nineteen years before Storm began to write his fairy tale, we have to assume that he had studied this account in full; and it highlights even more authentically the central moral idea of Storm's tale:

CHAPTER 3. CYPRIAN OF FOLK MAGIC

Cyprian was a student, a sensitive and skillful person by the way, but he attended the Black School in Norway and was therefore obliged by the devil to use his knowledge and his wonderful powers to do evil. This aggrieved him throughout the rest of his life, since he was heartfelt and pious, and so, in order to remedy evil, he wrote a book in which he first shows how evil is to be done, and then how it is undone. The book begins with an explanation of what sorcery is, and a warning against it. It is divided into three chapters, namely *Cyprianus*, *Doctor Faust*, and *Jakob Ramel*. The two last parts are written in characters which are to be Persian, or Arabic, or also occult signs. This book teaches blessing, conjuring, and wisdom, and all that is written in the fifth book of Moses 18.10.12. To what extent this book is printed one does not know, but handwritten copies hide here and there, having sanctuary among the people. The one who owns the book of Cyprian can never lack money, he can read the devil to himself and away from himself, and no one can harm him, not even the devil. But he who holds the book cannot get rid of it, for whether he sells, burns, or buries it, the book always comes back; and if he does not get rid of it before his death, things look bad. The only means is to write his name with his own blood and place it on a hidden stone in the church, together with four shillings in silver money.

— Thiele, p.92

There are several critical things to highlight here.

First, here is clearly an early blueprint of the idea which Storm worked into his tale: a sorcerer who turns out to be neither good nor bad but both, and who creates a product that is as perfectly ambivalent as he. An object—whether a grimoire or a magical mirror—that unites the forces of white and black magic, good and evil, in one occult device, which responds receptively to the way it is treated by the people who manage to obtain it. The device, and Cyprian, must thus be read as one: they are one living being, not a dead idea. They form a secret threshold which, crossed, can never be stepped back over. Or, as the wonderful Fritz Perls liked to say, "the only way out is through."

Second, there are still echoes of the original story of Cyprian of Antioch in this folklore, despite the one-and-a-half thousand years that stand between them. Both Cyprian of Antioch and Cyprian of the North have gained magical powers from 'the devil.'

Both of their stories are tales of compensation and redress. And yet neither of them can wash away the stains of their past. They remain dazzlingly occult characters, morally ambiguous, yet powerful and seductive.

Finally, we learn about how Cyprian works with his practitioners. Once they hold his grimoire in their hands or gaze deeply into his mirror, there is no easy way of turning back. To get access to the forces that Cyprian guards, one must strike a pact: "But he who holds the book cannot get rid of it, for whether he sells, burns, or buries it, the book always comes back; and if he does not get rid of it before his death, things look bad."

We have said that the body of Cyprian the Mage is essentially twofold in nature, made both from flesh and fiery light. In wanting to work with, and through, Cyprian the Mage, the practitioner has to accept that their own body will change as well. Isn't this the nature of any magical pact? The true *im-pact* lies not in offering up a drop of one's blood, but in offering access to one's blood. Like a genetic mutation, once we have bonded with a spirit, once we have invited it under our skin, it becomes part of us.

Here we also find the obvious parallel to the Iberian Cyprian. In the introduction of *The Great Book of St. Cyprian*, the legendary German monk Jonas Sufurino gives us his account of how he developed such a passion for this grimoire that he could never let go of it. With the voice of Lucifer we hear him say:

> This book, written in Hebrew, is the same one owned by great Cyprian, given him by me, when compelled by virtue of a powerful talisman which he owned. It served to acquire him the knowledge of True Magic and dominion over both spirits and people. By it he became all-powerful, as you will also, if you meditate upon and perform whatever this

> book contains. I must warn that it will not be parted from you; even should you attempt to burn it or cast it into a river, always you will return to find it in your monkish cell.
>
> — JSK *Testament*, Vol.1, p.14

Later in his story we learn that Sufurino was able to read the grimoire fluently, despite knowing hardly any Hebrew. All the sigils within it naturally revealed themselves to him and images of spirits stepped without hesitation out of its pages and talked to him.

> I found perfectly drawn a dragon and a goat calmly lying together. The goat had drawn upon its knees hieroglyphics that read *Arte*. As I looked upon this it seemed both strange and yet familiar; but a still greater surprise was awaiting me. The dragon and the goat became enlivened,

moving their eyes and increasing in size. Finally, leaving the book, they were prostrated before me; each speaking this in a human voice: "I am your servant, command and you will be obeyed."

— JSK, *Testament*, Vol.1, p.16

Now, let's make no mistake: what we find in this wonderful description is not a tale about a magical book. The book is used as a cipher for the magical process the practitioner experiences having successfully contacted their spirit-patron. Magic does not happen on the page, but on the senses of the mage, which, passing over a liminal spiritual threshold, begin to be altered and changed. It's precisely through this alchemical, deeply physical process that the mage becomes able to perceive and interact with beings that to outsiders seem as dead letters in a book.

Here we discover the real reason why the Black Book of Cyprian cannot be sold, burned, or buried once it has been opened: the magical book is a metaphor for the spiritual change that takes place within the body of the practitioner. Once we become companions of certain spirits, there is no going back to our old selves.

This is not to be read as invalidating the grimoire tradition. Quite the opposite: the story of "the spirit book that cannot be lost" needs to be read as a living testament to the importance of bringing the knowledge of spirits into our own body, of making it flesh.

Born only two years before Theodor Storm's death, Austin Osman Spare was the most prominent and prolific restorer of this knowledge in modern magic. He managed to derive his entire magical system of Zos-Kia from the interplay of void and flesh. Even though he was an accomplished artist and author, he built all his practice on the simple truth that it's the human body, not the book, that is the alembic of sorcery. (Grant, p.8)

CHAPTER 3. CYPRIAN OF FOLK MAGIC

This emphasis on the body and "making the flesh magic" is deeply ingrained in the tradition of Cyprian. From the gruesome physical details of his death (which we will examine later), to the adoration of his purported physical remains, to the prayers and spells that remember our magical saint, his forces are always anchored deeply in the chthonic realm.

A shining example of those prayers and spells is a protective one collected and published by a contemporary of Storm's, Adolf Wuttke, in his voluminous book on German folk magic:

> Three wicked tongues closed you, three holy tongues spoke for you. The first is the Lord the Father, the second is God the Son, the third is God the Holy Ghost. To you they grant you your blood and flesh, your peace and courage. Flesh and blood has grown on you, was born on you, and may (not?) be lost on you. Should a man have bewitched you, may you be

blessed by God and the holy Cyprian; should a woman have walked over you, be blessed by God and Maria's body; should a servant have challenged you, be blessed by God and heavenly law; should a maid have allured you, be blessed by God and the heavenly stars. The realm of heaven is above you, the realm of earth is below you, you are in the middle. I bless you from all sorcery.

— Wuttke, pp.162–163

Theodor Storm worked this aspect of our magical Saint beautifully into his modern tale, the construction of the sacristy having opened the wall behind which the magic mirror was hidden. Thus, accidentally, the boy in the background story was able to enter the secret space, glance into the mirror of Cyprian, and immediately fall sick. His body was touched by a magic he had no protection against, and his soul was pulled onto the threshold where life and death meet. And thus the magic of our saint becomes flesh. Whether it brings sickness or healing depends on the humans who shape and encounter it.

Early in his tale, Storm quotes the Brothers Grimm when he says that no kind of magic is good or bad, but depends on the hand that guides it. Such a belief, that any classification of magic into moral categories was doomed to fail, was deeply rooted in European folklore—and intensely fought against by the Church. People rightly understood that it wasn't the use of a particular category of plant, substance, or even spirit that deserved moral condemnation, but the underlying human intent that guided the practitioner's actions.

> The mark of sorcery I define as the evil intent to cause harm, and it seems to have emerged through an inversion of the use of secret natural forces to heal, almost as the devil emerged from the inversion of God. The particular applications of the

art as right and wrong, however, cannot always be clearly differentiated. Just as a herb, a stone, or a blessing can be curative in their effect, so they can also be corrosive. Use was proper and permitted; misuse was abhorred and punished.

— Grimm, p.924

The following quote from a male witch trial, close to the area where Storm lived but two hundred years earlier, exemplifies this belief nicely. Here a certain Hans Broecker, a local healer, said, after his arrest in 1645:

I became suspected of witchcraft and was taken to task by the authorities because I am able to invoke evil spirits to heal sickness.

— Schulte, p.174

And this is what the Brothers Grimm were wise enough not to mention in their encyclopedia: whether led by good or evil intent, no human hand will ever guide magic unless it has previously been stung by a spirit.

This was another conviction held by our European ancestors. The practice of sorcery or magic wasn't something one just picked up or dabbled in. It was an art, a calling in its truest sense, that people had to be empowered into. In the contorted voices of the witch trials, the devil himself initiated neophytes into this black art. But in the common belief of the people, things were much more profane. Due to its persecution by the Church, as well as its inherently practical nature, for centuries the teaching of magic had mainly been accomplished through an oral tradition. On an outer level, one had to train with a witch to become one. On an inner level, though, part of this training was the actual passing on of spirit-bonds or the empowerment to work as a line-holder of older lineages. That was how our tradition sustained itself in secrecy, by travelling through the very blood of those who practised it. One witch, one sorcerer at a time.

Ilsenburg & Olsborg

Cyprian of the Northern past

From flesh we move to earth. From the domain of the physical body out into the physical world. Now we must explore several geographical points in the Northern hemisphere related to our magical saint. In the first chapter we marked our saint's physical journey, and traced it all the way from the ancient Middle East to Rome, then further north to Piacenza at the feet of the Alps.

Now we have crossed this natural border made from stone and rock which eternally divides the southern and northern parts of Europe. The temperature has dropped, and lush pine groves have

Chapter 3. Cyprian of Folk Magic

Figure 3.1: The cloister of Ilsenburg Abbey as it appears today.

become cool forests and rolling hills. We are now in the old Germanic hinterland.

According to legend it was here, in a cloister at the foot of Mount Brocken, that *The Great Book of St. Cyprian* was first given to Jonas Sufurino by the devil in the year 1001. Surprisingly—or not—we see that this is the same year that the remains of Cyprian and Justina were transferred from Rome to Piacenza. Who was to say if it was the disruption of our saint's bones that had stirred his spirit and brought him back from the dead to speak to our German monk?

The area surrounding Mount Brocken is a landscape as deeply steeped in occult folklore as can be found across the Old World. The chances are high, therefore, that the real, anonymous author of *The Great Book of St. Cyprian* chose this area simply because of its sinister reputation. Placing his monk at the foot of Mount Brocken could have been a narrative decision to capitalize on its gloomy atmosphere.

CHAPTER 3. CYPRIAN OF FOLK MAGIC

However, if for a moment we wanted to assume that there is a grain of truth in the purported location where our monk received Cyprian's magical writings, then there is one obvious place to look. Nestled into the foot of Mount Brocken, on its northeast side, are the weather-beaten buildings of Ilsenburg Abbey. In 1003, Henry II awarded the area's former royal hunting lands to the Church, and shortly thereafter a Benedictine Abbey was erected. Yet even earlier, in 995, in a charter by King Otto III, we hear of a castle called Elysenaburg in the same domain (Sternal,p.27ff).

No other monastery of similar age was built so close to Mount Brocken. Close enough for a monk to climb to the top of the mountain and to return home in a single night.

Obviously the dates do not match perfectly. If we wish to consider this place the narrative backdrop for the emergence of Cyprian's book then either the book must have been backdated to match the year

1001, which is only eight years before the abbey's earliest mention (Sternal,p.27), or perhaps our monk only discovered his spiritual calling afterwards, and had been a visitor to the royal hunting lodge that had existed in this area before.

The former option seems more likely, as on the first page of his book Sufurino gives us some of his autobiographical background:

> I thus became monk in the monastery of Mount Brocken. Following my inclinations I asked for the librarian position and there, in its vast and ancient library, I isolated myself completely, spending years in the deepest and most mysterious studies. There were innumerable volumes there that dealt with the magical arts.
>
> — JSK, *Testament*, Vol. 1, p.12

If we assume that Sufurino's story did not take place at the turn of the eleventh century but at least fifty years later, then this description, notwithstanding some literary romanticism, could actually resonate with the truth about Ilsenburg's large library. Let's compare it to one of the few published accounts of the old library, one by Eduard Jacobsen in 1867:

> Of the even older abbot Herrand, the later bishop of Halberstadt, Winnigstädt tells us that the former even during his own lifetime had access to many sources that later were lost. In fact this "keen and learned man," who first had been *scholasticus* or master of the school at Ilsenburg and later became its abbot, had installed a kind of school of all sorts of free arts. He had every learned man follow his call and come to him.
>
> — Jacobs, 1967, p.336

Herrand was indeed one of the first abbots of Ilsenburg, and by 1090 he had already moved to Halberstadt as its bishop. Thus the above account must refer to the earliest days of the newly-founded monastery. Given also that only official church or aristocratic records have survived, the above description could indeed hint at a library that also contained books about magic. Furthermore, there is evidence that the library of Ilsenburg grew surprisingly quickly and remained relatively intact until the sixteenth century (Jacobs, 1867, p.335ff).

But as hard as we might try, the author of the introduction to *The Great Book of St. Cyprian* included too many obvious errors—even on the first two pages—for the credibility of his origin story not to suffer severely. Let's examine just two of them.

Jonas Sufurino claims to have joined the monastery at Mount Broken (JSK, *Testament*, Vol. 1, p.12). The author obviously didn't know that Mount Brocken had no name at all until the fifteenth century (Jacobs, p.8). As odd as it seems, given that Brocken is the highest mountain in North Germany (admittedly a very flat region), there is no evidence of it having any name in the Middle Ages. Though all the rivers coming down from it have specific names with mythical associations, the massive mount in their middle was nameless for most of its existence. So by definition no monk from 1001 or earlier could have referred to their home as a monastery at Mount Brocken.

"Rain whipped at the Gothic glass of the windows of the monastery," (JSK, *Testament*, Vol.1, p.13) the author tells us, somehow overlooking the fact that Gothic architecture emerged only towards the middle of the twelfth century.

To make things worse, as rich as the Harz is in magical folklore, and even specifically Ilsenburg Abbey (Kuhn, p.176, Pröhle, p.106), no matching legend or tale of a magical book received by a local monk has been discovered.

Thus, as we will see, we need to travel further north to encounter a place that allows for better trespassing between the realm of Cyprian the Mage and our physical reality.

In fact, from the central German region of Harz we must now return to its most northerly part, precisely where we met our novelist Theodor Storm before. Here we hear of an island where our mage was once put into exile by the devil himself:

> CCLXIII. Cyprianus—In ancient time on a Danish island lived a man by the name of Cyprianus who was worse than the devil. That was why, when he had died and gone to hell, the devil himself threw him out again and placed him on an island. It was here he wrote nine books, in the old Danish language, with sorcery and spells. Whoever reads all nine books has fallen for the devil. Of these originals a monk is purported to have made three

(or nine) copies; then they were cut into pieces and spread out across the entire world. One complete copy was owned by a count who lived in the castle of Plön. He put it into chains and buried it below the castle, as after reading the first eight books he was overcome by such a fear that he aimed to hide them from the eyes of the world. One of these books still exists in Flensburg. Individual spells from the books are still known to many old people. But if one wants to be initiated into them, one first has to forswear Christianity.

— Müllenhoff, p.192

When we read quotes like these, it's all too easy to forget where they originally came from. After all, folklore by definition is an oral tradition, even if elements of it ended up on the pages of books which we can quote hundreds or more years later. And this creates the impression of stability and continuity in a tradition which in effect changed with every peasant's mouth through which it travelled.

Even before the advent of the famous Brothers Grimm fairy tales in the first half of the nineteenth century, Romanticism was heavily in vogue in Central Europe. Faced with the brutal demands and deep social transformations brought on by emerging industrialization, authors and artists sought shelter and refuge in the romantic idea of a pure life amongst the folk people. The literary space that since the Middle Ages had been dominated by ballads and songs suddenly opened up to the vast uncharted territory of fairy tales, legends, and mythic stories, captured more or less in the vernacular of the people who knew them. Early collections of German tales and legends pointed to this very fact, the credibility of their stories advertised on a banner on their front page that read: "Collected from the mouth of the common folk." (Schmitt, p.25)

So how does this inform our reading of the quote above? Well, we now know that either a single person from the area of Schleswig or Holstein told this story to a folktale collector in the late eighteenth or early nineteenth century, or, more likely, several people from the same area told slightly different versions of this story to the collector, who then moulded all their accounts into one relatively consistent, short narrative.

It's this fluid process of emergence that helps us understand why several pieces of information are left out in Müllenhoff's account above, and why he mentions two geographical locations related to our magical saint: a Danish island as well as a castle by the name of Plön. Because the story was collected—or stitched together—from local people who knew the area very well, there was no need for them to stress that close to the village of Plön is a large network of vast lakes with several islands on them. They also did not need to mention that all of this area, which today belongs to Germany, was then Danish territory. In fact the castle of Plön itself once stood on one of these "Danish islands" in the lakes above which it now towers.

The particular island is called Olsborg and it is strategically well placed. Its location, roughly 490 feet from the shore and in open water, allowed it to be connected to the mainland by a wooden bridge, remnants of which were recently rediscovered. Its relatively small circumference, roughly five acres, made it easy to defend from all directions. After being a successful pagan settlement for at least two hundred years, the stronghold on this island was relocated to firmer, less marshy grounds on the current castle hill in 1173 (Bleile, p.112).

The people who settled on Olsborg remained heathens for a very long time. The first conversions in the area of Plön (Plune in older versions, from the Slavic term for ice-free waters) are only recorded in the tenth century. These were members of the Slavic

Chapter 3. Cyprian of Folk Magic

A lithograph of Castle Plön around 1864

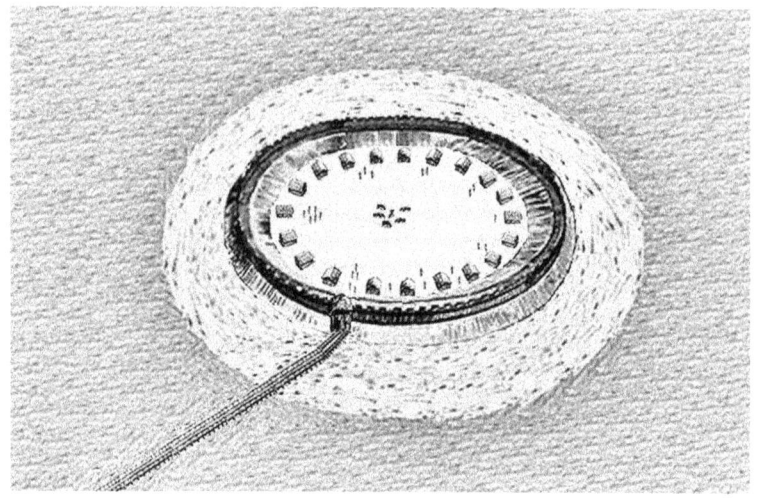

The ancient settlement at Olsborg, with its bridge connecting it to the mainland. Illustration by Ronny Krüger, public domain.

Obotrites tribe, and only two of the locations of their sacred cult spaces are known today. One of them was located directly on Olsborg.

The famous chronicler Helmold von Bosau (born ca. 1120, dead after 1177) captured his impressions from a trip to the area in the twelfth century:

CHAPTER 3. CYPRIAN OF FOLK MAGIC

> The Slavs had such awe for their sanctuaries that even in times of war they would not let their perimeters be stained by blood. (...) The Slavs hold many kind of idolatries, because they do not all agree in their superstitions. Some of them put on display in their temples fantastic images of their gods, like the idol in Plune which they call Podaga.
>
> — Helmold, p.190

Of the gender-neutral deity Podaga we learn more in Christian August Vulpius' large tome *Concise Dictionary of the German, Related, Neighbouring, and Nordic people*, from 1826:

> Podaga (...) His most distinguished temple was in Ploen, which is why Helmold calls him *Idolum Plunense*. He also had a temple in Lübeck and was not unknown amongst the Wends, Polish, and

Bohemians. With them, however, he was called Pogwist, Pogada: strong weather. Also as a female: Weather-Beaty, for support of agriculture, a god who gives grain and nutrition. But he was also a protector of fishing. His appearance was that of a human being, a pointed cap on his head from which emerged the two horns of an ox. In his right hand he held a cornucopia against his chest, in his left a wand. His dress only covers him up to his knees.

— Vulpius, pp.255–256

Now this may sound unlikely, but due to its marshy, remote, and undisturbed location, recent archaeological excavations from 2004 to 2007 rediscovered the remains of the original ritual pole on which this horned god once rested (Bleile, p.121).

CHAPTER 3. CYPRIAN OF FOLK MAGIC

Figure 3.2: The chapel at Plön castle as it appears today.

So not only do we know, now, exactly where the "Danish island" is that our magical saint once lived on, but we also have firm evidence of its use by a pagan cult—that Cyprian indeed once "shared it with the devil."

Again we stand at a crossroads. This time it is the crossroads of folk history and folk magic. For two quite different ways of reading Müllenhoff's account of Cyprian's legendary past in the German-Danish borderlands invite us to follow them.

If we follow the letter of the account, we must assume that one of the counts of Plön castle had a particular interest in the dark arts and ritual magic. Following this reading, we would walk down into the cellar of the castle and find that underneath its Eastern wing, instead of a basement, was a small chapel half submerged below the ground. Behind this chapel we'd come to a crypt which still holds thirteen coffins of the former counts and dukes of the castle. And maybe, this reading would suggest, this was the place where one of the ancestors tried to cut his bond with our magical saint and put his 'black books' into chains, burying them as far away from the public and himself as he could.

CHAPTER 3. CYPRIAN OF FOLK MAGIC

The other way of reading Müllenhoff's account is less literal, but still ancestral in nature. Here we would walk down from the garden of the castle all the way to the sloping bank. Then we would wade out into the cold waters, and swim further out, until we reached the ground and grove of the Isle of Olsborg.

Not with our human eyes, but with our spirit eyes, we would now see the crossroads on which we would be standing: a crossroads of blood and time, a place of power and collective memory in its purest form, not maintained by humans, but by the spirits themselves; not reached by plain directions, but by hints in half-forgotten stories, such as *The Tale of the Mirror of Cyprianus* and the distant memory of a heathen sorcerer who once lived on a Danish island. Here, on this small, unimposing island we might then see the Northern tradition of St. Cyprian blending with the blood of our own pagan past.

And through our mind's eye we'd see the shape of Cyprian the Mage become one with the many shapes of our ancestors, who erected adorned idols of the horned god and watched the sacred space with the blood they'd held for a lifetime, only to pass it on to us.

As we have already said, standing at the crossroads always comes with the privilege of choice.

Chapter Four

Cyprian of the Mysteries

First we explored Cyprian's moral ambiguity in depth. Following the translation of Storm's folktale we learned about our saint's strong affinity for the world of flesh. Most recently we encountered several physical locations in the Northern hemisphere which seem to allow for particularly easy congress between Cyprian's spirit world and our own.

In this chapter we'll focus on Cyprian's unique role as a patron of the craft of divination. To do this we will need to travel far back in time, but we shall begin at the point closest to us: the relatively young folk tale by Theodor Storm, *The Mirror of Cyprianus*.

Here the connection between our magical saint and divination is given in the most obvious terms: we encounter Cyprian in the form of a magical mirror, crafted by himself, adorned with magical powers and possessing the deep moral ambiguity that seems to sit at the heart of our ancient sorcerer's character.

Just like the Book of Cyprian that Julius Sufurino received from the devil, so the mirror that our countess receives from her sorcerer-friend is not a dead object, but a living, ensouled subject. By exposing oneself to it, by looking into it, the lines between future and present, inside and outside, subject and object, bewitcher and bewitched, begin to blur.

To understand how such magically charged objects actually worked, and how they were crafted by our ancestors, we'll first need to establish some foundations. These come in the form of a very basic understanding of divinatory practices, their techniques, and their prerequisites as we find them in our Western tradition.

CHAPTER 4. CYPRIAN OF THE MYSTERIES

The Many Faces of Divination

You develop from being an apprentice magician who does magic to being an adept magician who *is* magic: there is no need for tools or spells...The very presence and intention of the adept magician triggers change.

— Josephine McCarthy, in *Quareia*.

The history of magic in the West to a large degree is a story focused on the agency of spirits and devices. Most of our historical records, from grimoires to modern academic research, examine the kind of magic that is worked below the adept level. Here we find the magician embellished with lamens, rings, sigils, and books; with their bodies adorned with vestments, tools, and paraphernalia that all support the agency of particular spirits.

Each of these devices is a lesson in one's craft. When created by the magician and brought to life through spirit contact they can be powerful artefacts with authentic spirit bonds. However, each of these tools, robes, and rings also makes ties that confine us to a particular relationship in space and time. Like any gestalt, they require boundaries and energy if they are to be maintained and upheld. Many of them also are mutually exclusive and cannot be worked in harmony or in parallel, just as people can only speak one language at once if they wish to be understood by others.

The adept must move beyond this stage of working and learning through spiritual devices and pacts. The term 'beyond' has to be used with utmost care in this context, though, as it is easily read to imply judgement or differentiation in value: really it is meant in the sense of moving beyond a desert, mountain, or sea, which gives the journeyman access to new and different lands.

Of these lands, the territory of adept-level magic, our Western magical history speaks very little. Here the boundary between magic and mysticism begins to blur. The mage now walks empty-handed and naked. Rather than working through materials, substances, and symbols different from themselves, they work through the agency of their own blood, flesh, and spirit. They have essentially *become* magic.

We are faced with an interesting paradox here. Cyprian the Mage stands at the crossroads of these two kinds of magic. As a magician himself, remembered through his mythical biography and still active in the spirit world today, he represents the work of the adept. As a saint, an icon of veneration and a spiritual gateway, he has become a living tool in the hands of the mage below the adept level. How we choose to work with—or rather through—him and his legacy is entirely up to us.

However, the distinction between magic at adept level and below it, which is represented so well in the figure of Cyprian, is essential to understanding our tradition's records and practices of divination.

In his book *Inner Traditions of Magic*, William Gray memorably wrote that "we do not have enough power at our own disposal to do anything very wonderful." This is a very accurate description of the state of magical practice below adept level, as here the magician doesn't affect magic through themselves alone, but through the mediation of the spirit-empowered substances, tools, and devices surrounding them.

In contrast to this, when Aleister Crowley famously wrote "every man and woman is a star" he very much alluded to an adept-level way of working. However, as so often with The Great Beast's writings, he took great satisfaction in not making this explicit, thus sending generations of practitioners down an ego-driven rabbit hole when they mistook the significance of their mortal selves for the purity and permanence of a celestial star.

Now with this in mind, if we begin to trace the recorded tradition of Western ritual magic all the way back to the Ancient Greeks, the Chaldeans, or even the late Egyptian kingdoms, we quickly realize that the power of the mage resided in the versatility of their ability to connect with a wide array of spiritual beings. Folk magicians in particular, since the earliest times, have been utility players, or, in the eyes of orthodox religions, spiritual opportunists.

As explored above, the magic they performed was always an act of mediation rather than of performance. Whether they were mediating angels, demons, or deities, ancient ritual magic requires a spiritual being to work on behalf of the magician in a realm, and with means, that remained mostly inaccessible to the mage themselves. The mage and their tools in this context are mere gateways for the forces that pass through them.

Nothing illustrates this essential approach to magic better than the original idea of divination. The term itself is derived from the Latin word *divinare*, which translates means "to be inspired by a god."

Similarly the word 'oracle' goes back to the Latin verb *orare*, "to speak," and refers to a place where gods speak, not magicians.

> Immediately a second matter of dispute awaits us (...): whether a god, an angel, a daemon, or whoever (of the higher beings) always has to be present amongst the phenomena, revelations, or other sacred agencies (for these to take effect). Our response to this is simple: it is completely impossible for any divine work to be performed in the usual way without a member of the higher races being present as its custodian and worker. (...) This is because the human race itself is weak and small, only sees over short distances, and has an inborn vacuity.
>
> —Iamblichus, *De Mysteriis*, III 18, p.94

CHAPTER 4. CYPRIAN OF THE MYSTERIES

The interested reader is encouraged to explore the above-quoted section further. Iamblichus in his *De Mysteriis* goes to great lengths to explain the specific ways of working a divinatory act. We even find a chapter dealing with the particular question of whether a new and independent magical being is created through the interaction of theurgist and god or daemon while engaged in the act of divination (III.21).

However, if we step back from Iamblichus and our ancient Greco-Egyptian ancestors' theurgic knowledge, we discover four relatively distinct categories of divinatory practice. While each of them relied on a necessary divine custodian and worker to perform the actual act of divination, they can be distinguished by the way the theurgist operated towards this goal.

Professor of Classical and Ancient Studies Theodor Hopfner (1886–1946) in his epic double volume *Greco-Egyptian Manifestation-Sorcery*

(*Griechisch Ägyptischer Offenbarungszauber*) gives a detailed overview of these different forms of divination, as well as specific examples for each as recorded in the *Greek Magical Papyri* (Hopfner, Vol.II., p.119/120).

Again, through the lens of an adept practitioner such differentiation may seem not only artificial but also unnecessary, for adepts do not need to leverage exterior rituals, substances, or artefacts to connect directly with the divine and work with its ever-evolving patterns. Still, even for an adept there is value in Hopfner's categorization of divinatory practices, as it provides a historical lens and overview of how such practices have evolved and have been recorded in the Western (folk) tradition.

1. Theurgic Divination can be performed in two different ways:

   a) The realization of the divinity and its will is achieved by gnosis and the ecstatic ascension of the theurgist's mind and soul. (See: PGM M.IV 475 sq. Mithras-Lithurgy)

b) Alternatively, the appearance of the divinity within the human realm is achieved without any use of medium or substance of immanence, either while the theurgist is awake or within his dreams. (See, for awake: PGM IV 723 sq, PGM IV 3086–3124, PGM VII 913–928, PGM XII 224–230. And, for asleep: PGM V 384–453, PGM VII 694–708, PGM VIII 65–111, PGM XII 144–152.)

2. Magical Divination is the operation of bringing the divinity into the human realm by its being bound into a specific substance. This can again be achieved in two different ways:

a) By making the divinity appear in its true form either within the light of a flame (Lychnomantie) or within the surface of water kept within a cup, a bowl or cauldron (Lekanomantie). (See, for in flame: PGM IV 930–1114, PGM VII 549–587. And, for in water: PGM V 54–70, PGM IV 154–259, PGM VII 328–342.)

b) Alternatively, the divinity remains invisible but takes possession of a living being and communicates through them. (See PGM IV 850–929, PGM V 206–296.)

3. Goetic Divination, according to Hopfner's definition, is the act of bringing the divinity down into lifeless objects, and while it remains invisible it might move or change these objects in their appearance, sometimes even transforming them into their opposites. (See PGM VII 1–152.)

4. Necromantic Divination is the operation of bringing the divinity down into the body of the

dead, and while the divinity remains invisible it will speak and reveal itself through the agency of the deceased person's body. (See PGM IV 2140–2144, PGM IV 2006–2124, PGM IV 2145–2151, PGM IV 2186–2205, PGM IV 2205–2240, PGM IV 2152–2186.)

As we will see, the divinatory practice of particular interest for our study of Cyprian of Antioch belongs to Hopfner's category of Magical Divination. But before examining divination more specifically, let's continue to establish the basic requirements for such an act to be performed successfully.

Examining these four types of divination, we find that they all depend on a critical set of human skills. While the majority of practitioners indeed might not have enough magical power themselves to "do anything wonderful," it is certainly still within their reach to open gates and uphold such magical thresholds, and then for other beings to reach into the human realm and to perform things that *are* quite wonderful.

In essence, any act of divination depends on the mage's ability to do three things really well:

1. To deliberately establish contact with a designated spiritual being that has access to the information in question.

2. To uphold and maintain that contact for as long as it takes to transfer the necessary information from the spirit into the mage's mind.

3. To ensure that the contact remains pure and undisturbed from 'static noise' such as another spirit's influence or even the mage's own personal thoughts and imaginations.

If we reflect on these three criteria through our modern lens, what we really find here is the description of a clean communication interface. And that is precisely how our ancestors approached this problem. It is also how, over centuries, they evolved techniques and practices that did exactly what they were meant to do—as long as the magician knew how to apply them, which required not insignificant degrees of skill and care.

Example 1

Binding the Mage's Spirit into the Mirror

To illustrate this with a particular divinatory practice, we shall return to our modern folktale of Storms' *The Mirror of Cyprianus*. Early in the story we came across a description of a magical mirror created by our magical Saint:

> The gift I speak of is a *speculum*, a mirror in other words, crafted under a special crossing of the stars and at the most fortuitous time of year.
>
> — Theodor Storm,

The Mirror of Cyprianus

In this quote Storm is giving us a hint as to where he believed the most genuine description of a magical mirror is written. We can find it in the sixteenth-century book *Archidoxis Magicae Libri VII*, whose much-debated authorship is often attributed to Paracelsus. On the pages of its fifth and sixth books it provides a detailed description of how to create a *speculum* by utilizing specific astrological constellations.

According to Paracelsus' alchemical convictions, the seven metals were nature's most potent substances. Thus the instructions of the *Archidoxis Magicae* involve highly complex procedures to extract, purify, liquefy, mix, polish, and engrave the seven metals according to the nature of the work.

The most powerful substance of all can be obtained, according to Pseudo-Paracelsus, if all seven metals are brought together in one alloy by the name of *electrum*.

> Because if you bring together all seven metals according to the right manner and melt them into one, then you will receive a metal that contains and holds, hidden inside of it, all the virtues of the seven metals, and these you have here in this one metal which we call electrum. And it holds even more virtues: not only the virtues brought about by the pure metals as they hold their natural virtues, but in addition it holds supernatural virtues.
>
> —Paracelsus, *Werke Bd V*, p.318.

Thus the bespoke creation of a flat, metallic, polished surface of electrum is the main operation in the creation of a magical mirror, of which Pseudo-Paracelsus knows three different types, according to the astrological constellations under which they are completed. The first mirror reveals all human actions, the second all spoken words, and the third all written letters (Paracelsus, *Werke Bd V*, p.311).

As the rulers of the metals are also the rulers of the stars, it is no surprise that every single step of the work needs to respect specific astrological constellations. The melting of the lead depends on the auspicious position of Saturn, the melting of tin depends on Jupiter's positive position, iron on that of Mars, copper on that of Venus, silver on the Moon's, and gold on the Sun's. In addition, the correct position of the Moon and Sun need to be respected for each of the above steps, as well as the constellations under which the entire operation is begun and completed. A magical creation process that nevertheless "can be done within thirteen months," as Paracelsus reassuringly confirms.

The key to the operation, however, is that the theurgist binds his own *inner* stars into the object as well.

CHAPTER 4. CYPRIAN OF THE MYSTERIES

Paracelsus' interpretation of the mirror image relationship between Microcosm and Macrocosm was very literal: he believed every man to have mirror images of the planets within themselves. Thus, according to him, there was an inner as well as an outer firmament, each with its distinct dynamics and rotating constellations. He distinguished both by calling the inner or invisible stars within man the *Olympic Spirit*.

> In all these things know that during the creation of man the visible as well as the invisible body was created, and that both parts emerged from the limbo (i.e. corporal matter). The one part is earthly, the other celestial. The celestial part has its own effect and agency just as the earthly one. (...) And what the outer body is doing, these are actual works; but what the invisible does, that is just like the shadow of a body. (...)

These things are done by the Olympic Spirit who draws the shadow of all works of the earthly body. In the Olympic Spirit resides the *arte cabbalistica* with all its annexes, which kind of art proves that to the imagination of the one, who joins together all Olympic Spirits inside himself, many more things are possible. Because just as the visible corpora (i.e. the outer seven planets) can come together, so too is this possible for the Olympic Spirits of creation, who are the celestial body within man.

—Paracelsus, *Werke Bd II*, 232/233.

But what else is the invisible man other than the celestial body that is hidden in the mind and thoughts of the visible man, and which opens up through his imagination? As the celestial body can be inside man and through the Olympic

Spirit it can be led and brought into another (man), so it can be brought into the metals and put its impressions into them.

—Paracelsus, *Werke Bd V*, 322.

With incredible pragmatism applied, we find this unique concept put into practice in the *Archidoxis Magicae*. The book provides clear instructions on how to consider both the constellations of the outer stars as well as the ones of the Olympic Spirit of the operator. To this end the author advises the theurgist to calculate the precise day and time of his conception, not of his moment of birth (Paracelsus, *Werke Bd V*, p.313). From this he calculates his ruler of nativity, i.e. the star under whose sign he was conceived. For each step of the creation, then, both constellations are considered and matched. The outer ones are calculated by the visible stars, while the

Practica D. Theo
phrasti Paracelsi, gemacht
auff Europen / anzufahen in dem nechstkunffti gen Dreyssigsten Jar / Biß auff das Vier vnd Dreyssigst nachuolgend.

This book title page nicely illustrates Paracelsus's ideas about the inner and outer firmament.

inner ones are calculated by the constellation of the theurgist's ruler of nativity.

Earlier in our journey we mentioned that the magic mirror in Storm's folktale should not be considered a dead object, but a living being. We asserted that the *speculum* was a living expression of the sorcerer Cyprian himself, thus allowing us to strike a parallel between the virtues of the latter and the ones ascribed to the magical mirror in the novella.

Here, in Pseudo-Paracelsus' sixteenth-century instructions for the creation of an astrological mirror made from the seven metals, we discover the actual technique by which this magical act was meant to be accomplished, a way for the theurgist to bind his own mind, in the form of the Olympic Spirit, into the magical alloy that would become a mirror charged with supernatural virtues.

And the mirror of electrum is not just an individualized spiritual communication interface that allows direct contact with the seven planetary rulers.

By virtue of the substances from which it was created, it also wards off the interfering influence of any other spiritual entities that might distort the vision.

> It is further to be known that our electrum is abhorrent to all evil spirits, because hidden in our electrum lies the celestial force and the influence of all seven planets. Which is why the ancient magi of Persia and Chaldea have much done with them and found a lot within them. If I was to describe all these things to you here it would make for a curious chronicle, which I will omit because of the trouble, as the Sophist would proclaim me as the great arch-mage.
>
> — Paracelsus, *Werke Bd V*, p.321.

CHAPTER 4. CYPRIAN OF THE MYSTERIES

We have discovered a potent example of Magical Divination according to Hopfner's terminology. A magical device that required a huge amount of time, dedication, and skill to be crafted by its creator, yet by and in itself fulfilled all three criteria necessary for successful divination: the mage's ability to establish contact to the desired entity, to uphold it for the duration of the vision, and to keep the vision focused and pure from all other, possibly distorting spiritual influences.

Now we understand the true rarity of the gift our magical saint had sent to the countess. It truly was a gift created under the "rarest crossing of the stars," not only because our mage needed to consider the alignment of the planets above and below the night sky, but also the alignment of his own Olympic Spirit as it was bound into the mirror.

However, these intricate instructions to create a magical mirror as shared by our sixteenth-century Pseudo-Paracelsus are more than just another part of the web of Cyprian's tradition in the West. They are also a testament to the cunning complexity that likes to afflict our craft whenever it moves too far away from the true practice of the adept. Remember, just by kneeling with open hands and lifted gaze our fifth-century ancestors accessed magical gnosis in front of the painted burial wall of our saint's crypt in Rome. Fast forward a thousand years into the early Renaissance, and divinatory magic is confined to those who knew how to produce a seven-metal alloy over a minimum period of thirteen months.

This is not to say that such a mirror of electrum would not have magical qualities or that that its creation would not be a significant period of learning for one who mastered the complex processes of its production. But it has to be remembered that the further a tradition moves away from creating living, spiritual, firsthand experiences, the more anal, rigorous, and rigid it tends to become, and especially in preserving its history and protocol. Complexity, therefore, is often the hallmark of a dead or overly theorized path—just as much as forced simplicity can be the path of the fool.

In light of this we see that the magical mirror of Cyprian's tradition stands at a crossroads just like the magical saint himself. Whether it truly opens up a divine view into the future, or whether it simply reflects back a fool's gaze, we will never know—unless we dare to walk our own path.

Example 2

Working with the Empty Hand

We will now contrast the above sixteenth-century example of a highly complex divinatory practice with with one that couldn't be more different in its approach—yet it is even more closely related to our magical saint.

The following example was found in a rare eighteenth-century German book whose title translates to "One hundred and thirty-eight newly discovered and entirely well-tried secrets; or all kinds of magical, spagyric, sympathetic, and antipathetic wonders which once cost their owner a lot of money." This book, as its title states so eloquently, brings together precisely one hundred and thirty-eight distinct magical recipes, and contains a curious combination of basic folk medicine and general advise for magical conjurations.

After a severe warning not to meddle in Pseudo-Paracelsus' Olympic Spirit magic (secret 122, p.106) as well as a piece on the conjuration of the archangel Uriel (secret 123, p.107) we begin to read about our magical saint (secret 124, p.109):

> Of the Divination by the Cyprianum.
> In the time of a glorious then-ruling monarch, an Italian man came to a valet of the former and offered to show his

Chapter 4. Cyprian of the Mysteries

lord an arcanum by which he could know every day what the king of France did in his secret cabinet. His application was refused though, and he was given a thousand Reichsthaler ingratitude and as payment not to come again. The valet, however, who had far less integrity than his monarch, took the art for himself and seduced others with it.

It consists of this: that one has to take a young, chaste boy or a pure virgin, who shall conjure the holy Cyprianum to reveal to them in their hand (on which a paste of oil and grime has been applied) the Solomon.

Thereupon the red-bearded Solomon shall appear in their hand on his throne, holding a sceptre and dagger in either hand, and with a minister sitting to each of his sides. Once this apparition has come through, the young boy or the virgin shall hold their hand to their ear and ask what is being requested, and the spirit of Solomon shall reply.

— Karl Kiesewetter, *Faust in der Geschichte und Tradition*, Georg Olms 1978 (1893) pp.480–481.

It should be noted that only six pages later the same curious book tells of the art of creating magical mirrors. It references Pseudo-Paracelsus' approach of using metals, but dismisses it as suspicious for involving a spirit pact. Instead it suggests the practice of collecting the skull of a hanged man, crushing it to powder, dissolving it in an oil, and using it to anoint a steel mirror inscribed with magical sigils.

So while we are not far from the complex divinatory instructions we encountered in the previous chapter, in secret 124 we come across a divinatory conjuration that is impressive for its

CHAPTER 4. CYPRIAN OF THE MYSTERIES

stripped-down simplicity. Instead of thirteen months of hard astro-alchemical work or powdered skull-oil, all that is required is a young boy, some oily grime, and a prayer to Saint Cyprian.

> ...Onimantie or Onchomantie—which consists of anointing the inner palm or even the thumb's fingernail with a paste of grime and oil—in which, illuminated by the sun or a candle placed nearby, the visions appeared...
>
> — Karl Kiesewetter, *Faust in der Geschichte und Tradition*, Georg Olms 1978 (1893) p.477.

The contrast couldn't be more obvious. Instead of all those careful astronomical calculations and purifications, along with preparing and smelting the metals required by Pseudo-Paracelsus, here the mage literally works with *an empty hand.*

The frontispiece and title page of the book discussed in Example 2.

Chapter 4. Cyprian of the Mysteries

Hundert acht und dreyßig
neu=entdeckte
und
vollkommen bewährte

Geheimnüße

Oder
allerhand magische / spagy-
rische / sympathetische und
antipathetische

Kunst-Stücke,

Derer eines allein
den Besitzer viel Geld gekostet hat.
Bey dieser neuen Auflage
wiederum mit sehr vielen
andern Geheimnüssen
Und
einem vollständigen Register
vermehret / auch durchgehends
verbessert.

Franckfurt und Leipzig /
bey Carl Christoph Immig / Buchhändl.
1729.

Such a plain and straightforward approach to divination, however, does not necessarily represent a degradation in magical practice; it possibly represents the exact opposite. To better understand how the practice of divination evolved in the West from an historic perspective, let's turn to a short 1904 article by the Professor of Classical and Ancient Studies and Comparative Religion, Richard Wünsch (1869–1915). Even today academic studies on crystalomancy like to quote his brief summary and concise conclusions (e.g. Tuczay):

> But we have an even more ancient Roman informant from the first century B.C. in the scholarly antiquarian Barro. He reported that the king Numa Pompilius had conducted sorcery by water (Hydromantia) by making gods appear in the surface of the water who would reveal to him spiritual knowledge. According to him, this kind of sorcery

was invented by the Persians and in addition to king Numa had also been practised by Pythagoras. The account of Barro is a scholarly construction which we need to lead back to its actual facts. We may understand that a precursor to the magic by mirror was known to him, in the form of divination from the most simple mirror nature has given us: water. And this may be the surface of a flowing river or the surface of water contained in a bowl. Barro mentioned Hydromantia as it seems to provide a logical explanation for the legend according to which Numa received his revelations from the spring-nymph Egeria. (...) And that such an exploration of the future existed amongst the Ancient Greeks we learn from the Greek travelling author and ancient geographer Pausanias (born around 115, deceased 180 A.D.). In Patras, inside the sanctuary of the earth goddess Demeter, there was a spring which divined whether an illness would be cured or not. Into this spring a mirror was lowered on a string, so that it just slightly touched the surface of the water. Then one prayed to the goddess, offered olibanum, and gazed into the mirror: there one would behold the sick person either in full health again, or as a corpse. Here we indeed find both evolutionary stages of mirror-magic—a mirror made of water, and another made of metal—combined into one unified technique; and more importantly, linked to the divinatory power of the earth goddess. The faith in the prophetic knowledge of the earth used to be especially strong in Greece: the oldest

CHAPTER 4. CYPRIAN OF THE MYSTERIES

> Hellenic oracles were all consistently chthonic in nature.
>
> — Wünsch, pp.158–159

The further we push back in the time-line of our Western tradition, the more stripped-down the outer approach to divination seems to become. The intricate man-made mirror we know from our modern folktale about Cyprian is replaced with nature's most simple mirror, the surface of a river or lake. And the importance of particular magical devices is replaced with the significance of specific magical locations: a spring, a cave—a place connected to the chthonic forces of the earth.

But there is another significant connection between the above historical overview and the story of Cyprian the Mage. Interestingly, it is precisely the above-quoted Greek Demeter cult into which the young Cyprian was initiated. Here is what we read in his *Confessio* about his early magical years:

> ...at the age of ten years I bore the torches for Demeter and submitted to the white sorrow of Kore (i.e. Persephone), and I served the snake of Pallas on the Acropolis ... And what belongs to manlike divination, I apprehended from the Phrygians.
>
> — Nilsson, p.168.

Ryan Bailey, in his 2009 M.A. study, gives an even more pointed summary of our mage's many initiations:

> Cyprian is dedicated to Apollo as a child, joins the Mithraic mysteries, participates in the Stepterion and the rites of Eleusis, and spends an initiatory period on Mount Olympus. He then travels to Memphis and is initiated in the Egyptian *adyta* where he is privileged to visions of the variegated forms of demonic grotesquerie.

Chapter 4. Cyprian of the Mysteries

> After learning the mysteries of the Chaldeans, Cyprian's truly impressive occult *curriculum vitae* culminates in an encounter with the devil himself.
>
> — Bailey, p.2.

While the portrayal provided in the *Confessio* might be distorted by Christian polemic, it still gives a valuable impression of the intense nature of the original mystery cults. To fully understand Cyprian's role in divination we must understand the specific elements of these ancient mysteries experienced by our magical saint.

All mainstream religious rites today, however many people might participate in them, are echoes of what were once deeply personal and intimate experiences. In this sense, organized religion aims to freeze time, to mummify and expose mystical experiences that once were accessible only through a deeply personal journey requiring great commitment and mental acuity.

> Egyptians, Greeks, and Romans residing in Egypt during the Hellenistic and Roman eras cherished the ancient religious beliefs which for millennia had attached to their *terra sacra*. Abroad, those who had been initiated into the mysteries of Osiris continued to participate in his cult.
>
> — Delia, p.189.

As described in the *Confessio*, Cyprian lived during the high time of the mystery cults as they emerged in the Greco-Roman period adopted from the Orient. For the *mystes*, the initiates who had not only partaken in the public rites but proceeded into the deeper mysteries all the way to seeing the respective divinity face to face, the journey required significant dedication. Even before their first initiation—and they needed several—they had to commit themselves to extensive retreats, devotions, and preparations. The neophyte had to bow to the rule of the respective god or goddess they were asking for initiation, literally locking themselves up in the prison of their divine presence:

> ...even before his time (of the Roman historian Livy, 59 BC–17 CE) the term of consecration became intertwined with the word *sacramentum*. This postulates, as I said, that the service of the *myste* for their divinity was not only understood as a military service, but also that the first consecration was bound to an oath. (...) The time of probation, the desire to be sanctified, the bond for a lifetime, the vow of silence, all of this returns with Apuleius. For the time of probation, the ending of which was not determined by him but only by the goddess, he had to take residence in the area of the temple. As it seems, he was not allowed to leave it: whatever business has to be

attended in the city he has to direct through others. He takes the position of a prisoner of the goddess (...) He is pledged to asceticism—it is a taking on of the yoke. But a priest he still isn't.

— Reitzenstein, *Mysterienreligionen*, pp.194–196

Even in their slightly later Hellenistic form, these Mysteries were regarded not only as something deeply sacred, but also as an actual encounter with death in a sense so strict and real that it's unfortunate how many modern scholars prefer to misread it as a metaphor. By contrast, some of the Greek Magical Papyri from the same time, those that aim at the mystical ascent of the neophyte, prefer to transfer the actual magical experience from the human to an animal representative. What is done in actuality to a sacrificial animal was done, in a ritualized act, to the magician in more authentic forms of the Mysteries.

CHAPTER 4. CYPRIAN OF THE MYSTERIES

But why, then, was a personal encounter with death so critical to move through the innermost stage of the mystery cults? Earlier in this chapter, we established a working definition of what it means to practice magic at the level of an adept magician. We said that in each adept's life there was a threshold over which which they crossed. A period of time during which they bury all their treasures—their lamens, their robes, rings, wands, poisons, and daggers—and return them to the earth from which they came. Ultimately, they also bury themselves.

At the heart of the ancient mystery cults lay the idea of establishing a perpetual state of ritual gnosis: the idea of deifying the human practitioner and establishing a lasting, conscious bond between divinity and their own divine pattern. To achieve this in a ritualized setting in most mystery cults, extreme and extended forms of asceticism led up to a funerary rite of the *mystes*. Depending on the age of the cult, this could either be an actual death experience induced by blows to the head or poisonous potions, or a burial rite. These we still find conserved metaphorically in modern secret societies (Reitzenstein, *Mysterienreligionen* p.232). This process, known as *voluntaria mors*, "voluntary death," and the subsequent revivification by the hand of the god or goddess, was the central element of the deeper mystery rites.

> The god answered: "When I place my hand upon you, you are parting from your body." It says then: "He took off his gown in the Jordan, he took off his gown made of flesh and blood; he endowed him in a gown made of splendour and covered him with a pure and good turban of light." Then together they embark on the journey through the heavens which is often referred to in the death songs.
>
> — Reitzenstein, *Mysterienreligionen*, p.193, pp.231–232.

CHAPTER 4. CYPRIAN OF THE MYSTERIES

Once the human body had been left behind, the divinity was able to lift up the human spirit and guide it through the inner landscape. On this journey, the *mystes* was initiated into a series of foundational spirit contacts and asked for their blessing by means of prayers. According to Apuleius' rare description of a mystery cult rite, we know that the spirit of the practitioner visited the underworld, made contact with the dead, ascended to the planetary realm, and was initiated into the seven celestial powers (Reitzenstein, *Mysterienreligionen*, p.221).

In light of this, the story we encounter in Palladios' (364–430) famous *Historia Lausiaca* is of little surprise. Here we hear of the monk Serapion who is looking for the person most advanced in the divine practice of *ascesis* in ancient Rome. He hears of a devoted virgin who hasn't left her chamber for many years. Upon visiting her, he finds her resting on her bed, and enquires: "What do you do?" "I travel." "What are you?" "Dead." (Reitzenstein, *Mysterienreligionen*, p.206).

Thus the *mystes*, upon their return from the experience of the innermost mysteries, were called *morituri*, "death-facing ones." As we have seen above, according to his own magical biography, Cyprian made this transition early on in his life and became an adept, or a *mystes*, or whatever man-made term we choose to employ. Cyprian the mage was a living link in the chain of the death-facing ones.

Five hundred years after his death, and eight hundred years before his name would be conjured in the *One Hundred And Thirty-Eight Secrets*, we come across the oldest known depiction of our magical saint.

Ludwig Radermacher (1867–1952) in his important 1927 book *Griechische Quellen zur Faustsage (Greek sources of the Faust legend)* provides a full analysis of it, from which we quote the following relevant section:

Chapter 4. Cyprian of the Mysteries

The illustration referenced by Radermacher, Vie et Martyre de S. Cyprian, from H. Omont, Miniatures des Plus Anciens Manuscripts Grecs de la Bibliotheque Nationale du Vie au XIVe Siecle, P.XLVII.

The illustration we are inserting here is taken from the Parisinus gr. 150 and belongs to the end of the ninth century: therefore it is older than all of the known manuscripts of the legend, and yet it is clearly influenced by the legend. In the upper right we see Cyprian in his home, still wearing his pagan dress and, as it ought to be, without the halo of a saint. To the right of his feet we see a vessel containing magical scrolls and grimoires, behind him the spirit statue, and to his left a basin from which two figures are rising. Cyprian is occupied with a λεχανομαντεία. The globe on the table generally indicates scholarship.

— Radermacher, p.235.

At number twenty-seven in his comprehensive *Catechism of Divinatory Practices* from 1892, Gustav Gessman provides us with a precise description of the divinatory technique, referenced by Radermacher, called λεχανομαντεία:

> XXVII. *Lecanomancy* is a divinatory technique in which water is poured into a cauldron, then bars of silver or gold are placed into it on which magical conjurations have been engraved. These valuables would be offered more or less as reward to the demons if they would only reveal the future or things of interest. The prophecy was taken from the hissing and gurgling sounds in the water.
>
> — Gessman, *Katechismus der Wahrsagekünste*, 1892, p.64.

If we follow Radermacher's interpretation of this ancient image, we witness our magical saint caught amidst his own divinatory practice. His right hand is clearly stretched out towards the cauldron, indicating his engagement in the magical act. Depicting Cyprian

Enlargement of the previous image, of Cyprian and his magic bowl.

CHAPTER 4. CYPRIAN OF THE MYSTERIES

as a magical practitioner also makes sense in light of the rest of this small image cycle. As we follow it, we see the subsequent events of his *Confessio* unfold: his failed attempt to bewitch Justina, his baptism, and his martyrdom. Furthermore, such early iconography of our magical saint is evidence for his longstanding importance as patron of all diviners.

However, there is an alternative way of reading this image, one that Radermacher may have missed precisely by thinking of magic as an overly complex craft. What if the two statues in the basin were never meant to indicate figures leveraged in Lecanomancy? What if they were meant to depict Cyprian and Justina themselves?

In this reading of the image, we do not witness Cyprian practising Lecanomancy: what stands in front of him is a basin filled with nothing but water. And within it, our mage beholds the living image of fate in the shape of his and Justina's future martyrdom. Such an interpretation is much less daring than it might seem at first glance.

Towards the end of Cyprian's legend, we encounter a moment of Justina faltering in her faith. Cyprian has already been placed in a cauldron (or a large pan, in other translations) filled with pitch, wax, and fat, and set upon a large fire. Stepping closer, Justina hesitates, and is suddenly attacked by the "arch-evil snake, Cowardice" (Zahn, p.67). But Cyprian, the former pagan, reminds her of the faith she had once instilled in him, and asks her to come closer and step through the flames into the cauldron. Justina makes the sign of the cross and does as he advises. Through divine protection, both of them survive the ordeal, and are later beheaded at the shore of a river close by the city of Nicomedia (Zahn, p.70). From here it is that their remains, "more precious than stones or gold" (Zahn, p.71), are fetched six days later by the Roman seamen who secretly bring them to their ship and transport them to Rome, as we saw earlier.

It's the above detail of Cyprian and Justina's legend that explains why we encounter two

CHAPTER 4. CYPRIAN OF THE MYSTERIES

Cyprian and Justina in the cauldron, compared with the two figures Cyprian witnesses in his magic bowl.

iconographic traditions: one depicting their martyrdom in the flames, and another showing Cyprian either by himself or both of them united in the cauldron.

The fifth-century cycle of four images referred to above shows Cyprian alone in the cauldron, surrounded by flames. Many other depictions, however, resemble very much the scene that Cyprian witnesses during his divinatory act in the water basin. One of many examples can be found in a fifteenth-century mural in a small church in Austria dedicated to our saint, St. Zyprian in Sarntheim (Popp, p.255, image 71). There, on the northern wall below a sequence of seven scenes depicting Christ's Passion, we see a cycle of seven images illustrating the legend of Cyprian and Justina (Semper, p.257). Namely these are (1) the attempted seduction of Justina, (2) the baptism of Cyprian, (3) Cyprian's sanctification as bishop, (4) Cyprian bringing Justina into a monastery as abbess, and (5) the martyrdom of Justina and Cyprian. The final two images of the original cycle are lost today. However, according to similar cycles of the legend, such as the one in the Ex-Capella di S.Anna in the cathedral of Spoleto, it can be assumed that these depicted the flashing over of the flames onto the city governor as well as the beheading of Justina and Cyprian (Popp, p.94).

With this context in mind, we can decipher a different meaning of the oldest known depiction of

Chapter 4. Cyprian of the Mysteries

Cyprian's legend. Due to its iconographic subtlety, it's unlikely that the artist had ever intended for this meaning to be overt or immediately deduced by an uninitiated viewer. Rather, the artists would have intended it to be overlooked by the majority of the audience. This second, authentically occult meaning would have revealed itself only to a spectator who knew how to see it, or to one who used this image with the help of a teacher to learn how to see.

Let's remember that during the fifth century, sequences of images like these were meant to be accompanied by the spoken word of a narrator. They were illustrations that both sustained a somewhat orthodox narrative, as well as kept their stories alive to the audiences that would hear them told while watching them. Sequences of images like these were the blockbuster movies of their time—and one of the reasons why people came to attend services in the first place.

Now, let's also remember that the story of St. Cyprian was originally intended as a Christian polemic against the old pagan religions. However, as we established above, over time this polemic turned against itself when the figure of Cyprian became a Trojan horse that brought an entire pagan tradition into the canon of the Christian church. For the many magical practitioners amongst the early Christians, Cyprian's fate was not only of interest in light of his conversion to Christianity, but also in light of what happened before it.

As has been illustrated above, the key to this occult reading is to understand the two figurines in the water basin as a divinatory vision of Cyprian seeing his own fate. In this reading, then, we do not see a mage meddling with pagan demonic practices, but an adept magician looking into the death awaiting him. And at this very moment, as he sees the vision of his own martyrdom in the water, he realizes two things at once. First, that it is precisely within the experience of the flaming cauldron that his own faith will turn into flesh. And second, that his subsequent beheading will be its unavoidable consequence. It is the liminal moment of choice referenced earlier, the threshold over which every adept magician has to step. To accept the consequences of their own death experience in all its bittersweet power and potential, as a gift of a life that will materialize magic through their own body, yet a life that will also strip away all armour, all shielding, and all man-made protection. A life that will have to be walked naked, empty handed, amongst the flames, confined by the cauldron; without escape, but locked into the function and purpose that only they can fulfil.

If we accept this occult reading of the earliest depiction of our saint, we may continue with a second and final hint as to the true nature of the narrative the artist aimed to reveal.

Cyprian with and without his halo, left in his purported tomb in Rome, and right from the fifth-century illustration.

On the same fifth-century illustration, in the bottom left, we see Cyprian in the cauldron surrounded by black flames, and now crowned with the halo of the saint (or magical adept). We also see him looking directly at the viewer, with outstretched arms and open hands. This is the precise posture we came across earlier in our analysis. We might remember the fresco on the sacred wall in front

CHAPTER 4. CYPRIAN OF THE MYSTERIES

of our saint's purported tomb in Rome. Here we encountered a similar icon, possibly of St. Cyprian as a young man, with a particular ritual function indicated by his special posture:

> Thus it is perhaps not surprising that the central figure of the SS. Giovanni e Paolo icon has certain qualities of a vision. He ... becomes the earliest surviving instance of an icon image substituting for the devotee's personal vision of a saint in a shrine. Most remarkable is the clarity of the function of the saint in the icon. He is remote and otherworldly; he is to be venerated; and he prays in the orant pose of the catacombs. However, his eyes are not lifted to heaven but are directed out to the viewer. The icon is less a unique portrait of an individual saint than an object lesson in the function of a saint as intercessor.
>
> — Cynthia Hahn, *Seeing and Believing*, 1997, p.1094f

So now we understand: What we see on the fifth-century depiction of Cyprian is the image of a *mystes*, a "death-facing one" in the most literal sense. We see Cyprian at the very moment of his walking into his own death experience, while praying, and while becoming a chain in the link which we can use for our own prayers. In this image the artist reveals to us the liminal transition of a man of good faith into the empty-handed adept magician. In its most secret reading, then, the image becomes a living expression of the ancient mystery cults.

We see Cyprian as an adept, walking to his death with his hands empty and his eyes wide open. Cyprian has thus become not only the patron saint of diviners, but also the patron saint of adepts.

CHAPTER 4. CYPRIAN OF THE MYSTERIES

An anonymous painting of Cyprian and Justina in the cauldron. Cyprian wears an ill-fitting mitre. The man wearing green is the pagan priest Athanasius.

Conclusion

We have discovered that Cyprian is a mage of many faces. We can look at him (and work with him!) as the focal point of an entire literary genre; we can understand him as a somewhat secret map that leads us into the mythical landscape of our Western magical tradition; and of course we can see him as a spiritual patron and partner, an actual being that resides in the inner realm, waiting for us to approach its threshold and dare to utter our choices.

We have discovered that Cyprian will never judge us, the way we work with him, or the actual intent that brings us to him. He will appear as a book to the book-lover, as a magical tool to the mage, and as a living spiritual being to the adept. Which face we prefer to talk to, he couldn't care less. Because it's nature's way of working to offer all opportunities, all options, and all *consequences* to the race that carries the burden of free will.

Chapter Five

Cyprian of Cyprus

Companion of the Black Stone

A "rational" world devoid of peasant "superstitions" is, apparently, the world of bureaucrats and technocrats, the elite of Cypriot society. By denouncing magic in the name of Western science and rationality, the elitists are in effect denouncing the traditional Cypriot culture and social order in the name of an imported "modernity"...

— Argyrou, p.257.

The Great Female Divine

In the pre-Christian era, the term 'Cyprian' often had a very specific meaning. It was used to denote a pagan of a particularly lewd and licentious nature. Here is an historic explanation for this: according to Ancient Greek tradition, the goddess Aphrodite emerged from the Mediterranean sea at the frothy shores of Cyprus. Thus, one of her most important sanctuaries was established on the island at Paphos, which is the modern village of Kouklia, and it was actively visited and venerated for many centuries.

Excavations conducted at the site confirmed that it had in fact been used continuously for religious purposes from the third millennium B.C. until late Roman times. Compared with the significant age of the site, the Greek goddess Aphrodite is of relatively young origin. Long before her cult was introduced to the island, the sanctuary was dedicated to the great mother goddess Wanassa, or the "Queen of Heaven."

Chapter 5. Cyprian of Cyprus

Even thousands of years later, in the Greco-Roman period, her synonym was still simply 'Cypris,' the goddess of Cyprus. (Young, p.23, Dietrich, p.6.)

> The goddess embodied not only the sensuality known in Greco-Roman mythology but also incorporated aspects of fertility and military ferocity from Near Eastern prototypes of the goddess Inanna, with the result that she was revered for representing a spectrum of female qualities. The late writers Clement of Alexandria and Arnobius reported that the Paphian cult of Aphrodite included the giving of a model phallus and salt to initiates, the former clearly an expression of the sexuality/fertility aspect of the cult and the latter possibly referring to Aphrodite's birth from the sea. (...) In addition, votives showing

Phoenician traits indicate that the deity worshipped was also syncretized with the Near Eastern Astarte.

— Young, p.24.

Tacitus, Maximus of Tyre, as well as Philostratus in his biography of Apollonius of Tyana all mention the seemingly odd cultic image of the goddess venerated in her Paphian temple: instead of a human statue, a white pyramid of some unknown substance could be seen on her open-air altar:

The representation of the goddess has no human form: it is a rounded block, larger at the base and narrowing up to the summit, like a cone. The reason for this figure is unknown.

— Tacitus, after Antoniadi, p.178.

Chapter 5. Cyprian of Cyprus

Today we know that what Tacitus described was an *omphalos*, a ancient anaconic cultic object. Rather than really being entirely white, it is assumed that a black, possibly meteoric stone 1.22 metres tall had been covered by a white substance and shaped into a pyramid structure (Antoniadi, p.178). The stone itself can still be visited today in the Museum of Kouklia.

The Cyprian veneration of a large meteorite as the dwelling place of the goddess is a further indication of the old age and significance of this cultic site in pagan times. According to the patriarch Photius (A.D. 810–893) such meteorites were called *baetyli*, and Eusebiius Pamphilus (A.D. 260/265–339/340) further informs us that these artefacts were formed by one of the first gods, Uranos, who thus "created souled stones" (Antoniadi, p.177).

Ultimately the cultic site at Palaiapaphos became so well known that ancient writers would use its name as a literary reference: they could simply assume that the reader would know of the richness of the cult and its related rites, either from firsthand knowledge or purely by reputation (Young, p.26). If we were to trust these Greek and later Christian sources, the rites at Palaiapaphos consisted mainly of sexual and divinatory practices:

> Although couched in metaphoric language, the references allude to ritual bathing, the use of perfumes and oils, incense burning, ritual prostitution, and divination as aspects of the cult's practices at Palaiapaphos. The most notorious of the cultic activities in honour of Aphrodite at Palaiapaphos was ritual prostitution, as evidenced primarily in late expressions of Christian outrage but also implied in an early reference by Herodotus.
>
> — Young, p.27.

"Stone representing Aphrodite at Kouklia." Photograph by Rjdeadly, 2017. (CC BY-SA 4.0)

Now we understand why the term 'Cyprian' in the first centuries A.D. was broadly used to refer to pagan magicians and their 'licentious' rites.

In light of this, the word 'Cyprian' in the title Cyprian of Antioch, though usually read as meaning someone who had originally come from Cyprus, is more likely a stylistic device to refer to the extremely depraved nature of our antihero. Any colourful story involving virgins, demons, love, and the ultimate conversion to the true, i.e. Christian, faith would have been worthwhile telling anyway in the early centuries A.D.. But making a 'Cyprian' magician convert to Christianity would have raised the stakes even further: it would make for the most audacious example of a young Christian virgin overpowering the age-old pagan gods in the form of their human agent.

However, there is still more to discover about the nature of our magical saint amongst the cult's ruins in Cyprus. In fact, if we stopped here we'd likely miss the unveiling of the most essential aspect of his magical character. One that was only hinted at before. One that is easily lost in the bright light of our saint's powerful presence. Here is how the story continues:

Whether we look into the mythology of the Near East or at Greco-Roman myths, the original goddess who represents nature's fertility was often associated with a male consort. In the realm of Aphrodite, this companion role is taken mostly by either Apollo or Adonis. The latter is referred to by Ovid as the son of the mythical Cinyras, the ancient king of Cyprus.

Now, we find the myth of Adonis in many ancient sources and in several variants, as for example in Theocritus' *Fifteenth Idyll* from the third century B.C., or in the tenth book of Ovid's *Metamorphoses*. With obvious reference to the Egyptian divine relationship between Isis, Horus, and Osiris, we can identify the following core patterns of the myth:

King Cinyras' daughter Myrrha is overcome by an unnatural lust for her own father, lies with him, and then, regretting her deed, asks the gods to change her into something other than human. The gods assent, and turn her into a tree; so we hear about the mythical origin of the famous Myrrh tree.

Her unborn son, however, is still inside her womb. Thus, when the time comes, he breaks free from the tree, causing it to rain down its resinous sap, upon which he feeds.

Here the myth splits into two versions. According to the first, the goddess Aphrodite, impressed by the baby's beauty, shelters it and entrusts him to Persephone. She falls for the boy's beauty as much as Aphrodite, and refuses to return him. The dispute is settled by Zeus, who rules that Adonis will spend one third of his time in the underworld at Persephone's side, a second third with Aphrodite, and the third third as he chooses. Adonis chooses Aphrodite, and so the fertility goddess and her male companion are united (aligned to Greece's seasonality and its warm climate) for two thirds of the year, while the potent, male power of nature withdraws into the underworld with Persephone for the remaining third.

The alternate version of the myth speaks of the following events:

> The handsome youth was taken by Aphrodite as her lover, but after he was accidentally killed by a boar, she searched for his body and found it (significantly) in a sanctuary of Apollo in Cyprus. Although Zeus would not restore him completely to life, she persuaded him at least to permit him to accompany Persephone in her half year on earth and half in the underworld.
>
> — Young, p.28.

Our Cyprian goddess, therefore, had a main male companion with a rather ambivalent nature: both dead and alive, and equally at home by the hearth of the living and in the darkness of the underworld. In light of our goddess' cult object, the ancient black rock which is possibly of meteoric origin, Adonis' role, however, gains further importance. He is also the human agent of female divinity. And, at least according to one version of the myth, it is her love that initially led to his death and later to his resurrection.

The male consort of our lady Cypris, i.e. her companion 'Cyprian' in the most literal sense, forms the human interface who bridges the powers of the female divine as ensouled in the black rock. He is the adept mage who accepts the annually recurring passage through death in order to rebalance his male powers and become the generative principle that upholds and rebalances nature. And yet from the perspective of his cult's practitioners, Cyprian-Adonis is a portal that leads both ways: into death as much as into life.

In light of this mutual dependence of Cypris-Aphrodite and Cyprian-Adonis, it is of little surprise that recent excavations have identified, on a hill on the island of Cyprus, the ancient remains of a sanctuary dedicated to Apollo and Adonis:

> Recent excavations at ancient Idalion (modern Dhali) located at a halfway point from the mountain mines and the coastal shipping ports have discovered a "temple of Apollo" on the lower slopes of the eastern acropolis of the city that was crowned by a larger "temple of Aphrodite." Interestingly, this hill is also traditionally associated with the story of Adonis, whose name probably derives from the Semitic title "Adon" meaning "lord."
>
> — Young, p.28.

The temples of Apollo and Adonis were not, however, the first to accompany the great mother goddess Wanassa in the black rock on the island of Cyprian. In 1948, excavations discovered a significant Bronze Age (third millennium B.C.) temple complex at Enkomi. In a two-storey underground shrine the central statue of a male, standing figure was found, dressed in a kilt and wearing a conical headdress composed of two arching steer horns.

> That this horned figure represented the sanctuary's central cult image is inferred not only from the remains of sacrificial offerings and libations discovered in adjacent rooms, but also from the specific presence of bovine and horned cult objects found among the scattered debris. (...) The statue had been removed from its original setting and reinstalled following a sizeable earthquake.
>
> — Kotansky, p.331.

> The 'Horned God' of Enkomi represents the earliest known version of the male consort to the formless divine mother goddess that was worshipped on the island. His roots thus stretch back deep into time and far beyond the emergence of the Greek religion. We hear echoes of the Syrian god Reshef, possibly imported to ancient Bronze Age Cyprus by the Phoenicians, and developed into a local patron god who ruled equally over death and healing.
>
> — Dietrich, p.2.

More important for our study than the origins of the 'Horned God,' though, is the fact that for at least three thousand years an unformed female power was revered in combination with a male agent. Whether bringing death or healing, the female power provides substance and force, while the male agent directs it into patterns and shapes.

The relationship of the female and male deities made evident in the topographical location of their sanctuaries at Idalion with its visible association of two ritual sites, that of the "Lady" and that of the "Lord," shows the general association of the "Great Goddess" and her consort, together representing the male and female aspects of natural and human fertility through their *hieros gamos*.

— Young, p.29.

At the Cypriot sites of Palaiapaphos and Rantidi there was worship of the female and male forces of natural fertility and sexuality as far back as the third millennium B.C., continuing in various forms into the late Roman era.

— Young, p.44.

Conclusion

So maybe what is hidden in the story of our magical saint is more than just a literary reference to the lewdest sort of magicians of the ancient world. Maybe Cyprian and Justina themselves are the echoes of a much older cult, the remains of which would have still been intact on the island of Cyprus in the fourth century when their original legend was written.

Just as the original stone of Cypris-Aphrodite was white, so the shape of our virgin Justina is formless and pale in the original three books of the legend. While ultimately the focus of the legend and significantly more powerful than our male magician Cyprian-Apollo, her character stands out by its marked simplicity and lack of profile, both literary and real.

Yet Justina singlehandedly overcomes the attempts of Cyprian to dominate her, to turn her into the object of his desire and lust. And just as

Apollo is both saved by Aphrodite and later killed by her love, so Cyprian is first saved by Justina and later put to the sword for their shared new faith.

In an earlier chapter we discussed the difference between a mage and an adept magician. The importance of having walked through death stood out as a marked criterion for the latter kind of practitioner. We identified Cyprian of Antioch as such an adept magician, and explored how this had informed his non-dual approach to life, turning him into a seemingly inhuman saint, a giver of poison as much as of life, a bringer of death as much as of healing. A figure that wears the devil's skin right under his own.

What we have discovered in this final chapter is a possibility of much more than this. Rather than focusing our investigation on Cyprian himself and his own magical DNA, we have begun to look at what kind of force he might be able to mediate into our own lives. Rather than asking "who is he?" we might now rather want to ask "what is he bringing through?"

Isn't this the problem with most men in the end? In taking too much time to look at their projected, grand selves, it is all to easy to forget to look beyond them. And there, in the background of our magical hero, we discover the real meaning of his legend: Justina. Not a pale straw man promoting the newly emerging Christian faith, but, if read through a mythic lens, the ancient echo of the fertile mother goddess herself.

Justina is thus a memory-anchor of the formless being from the depths of the earth—or from the stars, if we'd like to view her black stone as meteoric—which quintessentially transcends the human realm. A form of female divinity which can become flesh only by the unconditional agency of her male companion.

Her companion is Cyprian-Apollo, who in a continuous cycle traverses death and life only to turn himself into a bridge that upholds her anaconic forces and enables them to merge into fertile seeds of substance.

In the first chapter of this book, we began our journey by examining Bernard of Chartres' metaphor that we are nothing but dwarfs standing on the shoulder of giants. We discovered the unique form of Platonism that he had developed. Building on Plato's original ideas, he formed his own natural philosophy which postulated a unique, mediating principle between the timeless world of the ideas and creation as we know it. Bernard of Chartres called these "shapes of emergence" or *formae nativae*. In the words of this twelfth-century philosopher, that is precisely how we can now imagine the function of Cyprian of Antioch. Cyprian is an adept magician, a man who walked through death and back with one purpose in his mind: to become a *formae nativae* to Cypris, the great female divine.

At the beginning our exploration we also called out the popular opinion that the story of our lady Justina and Cyprian was nothing more than a piece of early Christian propaganda. As we have illustrated in these pages, we beg to differ.

We'd instead like to think of this fascinating story as a triple Trojan horse.

On its most superficial level, it is the story of a most powerful Christian virgin overcoming the lewdest of all magicians.

Underneath this thin veneer, and inside the first layer of the horse, the legend becomes a memory-anchor for all the pagans and heretics within the newly emerging Church, allowing them to remember one of their own in the figure of Cyprian of Antioch.

And looked at from this angle, the resurgence of the cult of Cyprian of Antioch is indeed an equally powerful, as well as ironic, emerging trend. It is powerful in that it allows many Western magicians finally to reconcile the seeming chasm between their spiritual roots and the Christian communities in which they were brought up. And it is ironic in that it is a story that, having once belonged to an

Both these etchings are by the Dutch artist, Sébastien Le Clerc (1637-1714), and are from the late seventeenth or early eighteen century. They were loose prints, not bound into a book.

Chapter 5. Cyprian of Cyprus

The first etching actually depicts Cyprian of Cathargo, not Cyprian of Antioch. They are a good example of how these two separate Saint Cyprians have often been confused throughout the centuries.

orthodox Christian canon, has at last brought pagan magic back into their crumbling churches: rather than imbuing them with tears and mumbled prayers, secret spiritual fires are lit again and old statues are once more brought to life.

However, the Mysteries by nature like to escape the limelight. They like to stay hidden. And indeed, faced with the current avalanche of books and the emerging magical industry surrounding Cyprian of Antioch, it is easy to overlook the third, innermost chamber of this Trojan horse. Here, in the silent heart of the story, we encounter not Cyprian, but the force that upholds him: the ancient, formless female divine, Cypris-Wanassa, and her magical companion.

Eliphas Levi, in all his eighteenth-century Romanticism and with the force of a broken heart, liked to repeat the purported Egyptian saying: "Osiris is a black god." Well, in this vein we should perhaps say from now on: "Cyprian of Antioch is a black god. And he is hiding a black stone within him."

Afterword

So where do we go from here?

Let me try to make this simple. You have a choice to make.

Each facet of our magical saint's heritage and life which we have examined can be seen through a twofold lens: as artefacts of *veneration* or *inspiration*.

You can turn yourself into a pilgrim following in his tracks, and visit Rome, Milan, and even Syria if you dare. You can search for his tomb, for the casket that once carried his bones, and intone the conjurations and prayers that appeared under his blessing. In this case you are not following his path, but you are attaching yourself to him. You are feeding the gate which he is, and upholding it with your attention, adoration, and acts. In return you'll get a fair deal, if that is what you are after. You'll receive his empowerment, and he might mediate access to other beings on your behalf. That's how you perform spells under the guidance of our magical saint.

But there is also an altogether different option. Remember, Cyprian *is* the crossroads: these are the kinds of choices that we only get to make *once*. So rather than taking the path of veneration, you could view each episode of this madman's life as inspiration for your own. Instead of attaching yourself to Cyprian, you could view his stories as the experiences of a fellow traveller, as someone who has come before you, who might inspire you to carve out your own path.

It's the same with all saints, heroes, and magicians: mostly people need them once they have given up all hope of becoming one themselves.

Now, for the few who truly choose the second option, my advise is most likely useless; but it is, at least, simple:

Begin with the end in mind.
Begin with finding your own black stone.

Bibliography

Ali, ConjureMan. Saint Cyprian: Saint of Necromancers, Hadean Press 2011

Anonymous. Ludwig von Cyprian—des Weltweisen Höllenzwang, Hamburg (1509) ?

Antoniadi, E.M.. On Ancient Meteorites, and on the origin of the crescent and star emblem; in: The Journal of the Royal Astronomical Society of Canada, Vol.XXXIII, No.5m p.177-184

Argyrou, Vassos. Under a Spell: The Strategic Use of Magic in Greek Cypriot Society; in: American Ethnologist, Vol. 20, No. 2 (May, 1993), pp. 256-271

Artiss, David. Theodor Storm: Studies in Ambivalence, John Benjamins Publishing Company 1978

Bailey, Ryan. The Confession of Cyprian of Antioch: Introduction, Text, and Translation, Montreal 2009

Basset, Rene. Les Apocryphes éthiopiens traduits en français par Renee Basset, VI: Les prières de S.Cyprien et de Théophile, Paris 1896

Bilabel, Friedrich & Grohmann, Adolf. Griechische, Koptische und arabische Texte zur Religion und religiösen Literatur in Ägyptens Spätzeit, in: Veröffentlichungen aus den badischen Papyrus-Sammlungen 5, Heidelberg 1934

Bleile, Ralf. Das Projekt Olsborg: Untersuchungen auf einer Insel im Großen Plöner See. `http://www.ufg.uni-kiel.de/en/staff-directory/professors/ulrich-muller/projects-1/olsburg`

Brüning, Fritz. Die alchemistischen Druckwerke von der Erfindung der Buchdruckerkunst bis zum Jahre 1690, Walter de Gruyter 2004

Cummins, Alexander & Hathaway Diaz, Jesse & Zahrt, Jennifer (Editors), Cypriana: Old World, Rubedo Press 2016

de Mattos Frisvold, Nicholaj. St. Cyprian & the

Bibliography

Sorcerous Transmutation, Hadean Press 2013

Delia, Diana. The Refreshing Water of Osiris, in: Journal of the American Research Center in Egypt, Vol. 29 (1992), pp. 181-190

Dietrich, B.C.. Some Evidence from Cyprus of Apolline Cult in the Bronze Age; in: Rheinisches Museum fur Philologie, Neue Folge, 121. Bd., H. 1 (1978), pp. 1-18

Frankfurter, David. Demon Invocations in the Coptic Magical Spells, p.6/7

Gessmann, Gustav. Katechismus der Wahrsagekünste mit besonderer Berücksichtigung der Punktierkunst, Berlin 1892

Gratopp Karl. Volkspoesie und Volksglauben in den Dichtungen Theodor Storms, Rostock 1914

Griffith, F.Ll.. Herodotus II. 90. Apotheosis by drowning, in: Zeitschrift für Ägyptische Sprache und Altertumskunde Vol. 46, 1910, p.132-136

Grimm, Jakob. Deutsche Mythologie, Vol. II, Berlin 1875 (1835)

Grohmann, Adolf. Studien zu den Cyprianusgebeten, in: Wiener Zeitschrift fur die Kunde des Morgenlandes, Vol. 30 (1917/1918), pp. 121- 150

Hahn, Cynthia. Seeing and Believing: The Construction of Sanctity in Early-Medieval Saints' Shrines, in: Speculum, Vol. 72, No. 4 (Oct., 1997), pp. 1079-1106, University of Chicago Press 1997

Helmold von Bosau, Chronik der Slaven, Leipzig 1894

Hopfner, Theodor. Griechisch Ägyptischer Offenbarungszauber, Band 1, Amsterdam 1974

Hopfner, Theodor. Griechisch Ägyptischer Offenbarungszauber, Band 2, Amsterdam 1983

Hopfner, Theodor. Iamblichus - Über die Geheimlehren, Georg Olms 1987

Jacobs, Eduard. Der Brocken in Geschichte und Sage, Halle 1879

Jacobs, Eduard. Über die ehemalige Bibliothek und

das Archiv des Klosters Ilsenburg, Halle 1867

Jensen, Brian Møller. The Story of Justina and Cyprian of Antioch as told in a Medieval Lectionary from Piacenza, Stockholm University 2012

Kiesewetter, Karl. Wer ist der Mann? Ein theurgisches Rätsel; in: Hübbe-Schleiden, J.U. (Ed.). Sphinx, III. Jahrgang 1888, Sechster Band, Gera 1888, pp.184-231

Kotansky, Roy & Spier, Jeffrey. The "Horned Hunter" on a Lost Gnostic Gem; in: The Harvard Theological Review, Vol. 88, No. 3 (Jul., 1995), pp. 315-337

Kuhn, Adalbert & Schwartz, Wilhelm. Norddeutsche Sagen Märchen und Gebräuche, 1848

Leitão, José. The Book of St. Cyprian: The Sorcerer's Treasure, Hadean Press 2014

Leitão, José. The Immaterial Book of St. Cyprian, Rubedo Press 2017

Maggi, Humberto. The Book of St. Cyprian,

Nephilim Press 2017

Martène, Edmond & Durand, Ursin. Thesaurus Novus Anecdotorum, Tomus Tertius, Paris 1717

Michel, Karl. Gebet und Bild in frühchristlicher Zeit, Leipzig 1902

Moßner, Tamara & Nauerth, Claudia. Das Zauberbuch des Cyprianus, in: Agyptische Magie im Wandel der Zeiten, Heidelberg 2011

Müllenhoff, Karl. Sagen, Märchen und Lieder der Herzogthümer Schleswig Holstein und Lauenburg, 1845

Nilsson, Martin. Greek Mysteries in the Confession of St. Cyprian, in: The Harvard Theological Review, Vol. 40, No. 3 (Jul., 1947), pp. 167-176

Polotsky, Hans Jakob. Zu einigen Heidelberger koptischen Zaubertexten, in: Orientalia, NOVA SERIES, Vol. 4 (1935), pp. 416-425

Popp, Sigried. Die Fresken von St. Vigil und St. Zyprian Studien zur Bozner Wandmalerei um 1400, Dissertation, Berlin 2003

Pröhle, Heinrich. Unterharzische Sagen, 1856

Radermacher, Ludwig. Griechische Quellen zur Faustsage - Der Zauberer Cyprianus, die Erzählung des Helladius Theophilus, Wien 1927

Reitzenstein, Richard. Cyprian der Magier; in: Nachrichten von der Königlichen Gesellschaft der Wissenschaften zu Göttingen, 1917, pp. 38–79.

Reitzenstein, Richard. Die Hellenistischen Mysterienreligionen, Darmstadt 1966

Reitzenstein, Richard. Zu Cyprian dem Magier, in: Weinrich, Otto (Ed.), Archiv für Religionswissenschaft 20, Leipzig and Berlin 1920–1921; pp. 236–37

Ryssel, Victor. Der Urtext der Cyprianuslegende, in: Brandl, A. & Tobler A. (Ed.), Archiv für das Studium der neueren Sprachen und Literaturen, Band 110, Braunschweig 1903

Schaeffer, Claude F. & A. Enkomi Alasia. In: Syria. Tome 29 fascicule 3-4, 1952. pp. 333-336

Schermann, Theodor. Die griechischen Kyprianosgebete, Oriens Christianus III, 1903, p.303-323

Schmitt, Christoph. Homo Narrans: Studien zur populären Erzählkultur, Waxmann 1999

Schulte, Rolf. Man as Witch—Male Witches in Central Europe, 2009

Semper, Hans. Über die Wandgemalde der St. Vigiliuskapelle des Schlosses Weineck bei Bozen

Young, Philip. The Cypriot Aphrodite Cult: Paphos, Rantidi, and Saint Barnabas; in: Journal of Near Eastern Studies, Vol. 64, No. 1 (January 2005), pp. 23-44

Skinner, Stephen & David, Rankine. The Grimoire of Saint Cyprian - Clavis Inferni, Llewellyn Worldwide 2010

Sternal, Bernd. Burgen und Schlösser der Harzregion, Band 5, 2014

Stratton-Kent, Jake. Geosophia: The Argo of Magic, Volumes I and II Scarlet Imprint 2010

Stratton-Kent, Jake. The Testament of Cyprian the Mage, Volumes I and II, Scarlet Imprint, 2013

Thiele, J.M.. Danmarks Folkesagn, Vol.II, Copenhagen 1843

Tuczay, Christa. Die Kunst der Kristallomantie und ihre Darstellung in deutschen Texten des Mittelalters, in: Mediaevistik, Vol. 15 (2002), pp. 31-50

Voskos, Ioannis & Knapp, Bernard. Cyprus at the End of the Late Bronze Age: Crisis and Colonization or Continuity and Hybridization?; in: American Journal of Archaeology, Vol. 112, No. 4 (Oct., 2008), pp. 659-684

Wimmer, Erich. Cyprianus, in: Ranke, Kurt. Enzyklopädie des Märchens, Band4: Chronikliteratur - Engel und Eremit, de Gruyter 1981

Wuttke, Adolf. Der deutsche Volksglaube der Gegenwart, Berlin 1869

Wünsch, Richard. ein Odenwalder Zauberspiegel, in:

Strack, Adolf; Hessische Blätter für Volkskunde, Band III, Leipzig 1904

Zahn, Theodor. Cyprian von Antiochien und die deutsche Faustsage, Erlangen 1882

www.ingramcontent.com/pod-product-compliance
Lightning Source LLC
Chambersburg PA
CBHW041308240426
43661CB00038B/1468/J